Chaos and the Automaton

e-flux

Chaos and the Automaton

Franco "Bifo" Berardi

Edited by Andreas Petrossiants

Printed and Distributed by
the University of Minnesota Press

CONTENTS

INTRODUCTION
Interview with Andreas Petrossiants

2023

Andreas Petrossiants The historical breadth of these essays, both in the time of their writing and in their references, point to changes in regimes of production and labor, alternative and "counter-cultural" forms of life and their recuperation, as well as cycles of revolutionary struggle. Reading them, one can trace certain lines of thought from reactions to industrial expansion and to its decay through post-Fordist restructuring as well as the socio-cultural foundations to neoliberal ideology and its mass cognitive aftershocks. What are some of the throughlines you follow between 1968 in Paris, '77 in Italy, 2001 in Zuccotti park, and so on?

Franco "Bifo" Berardi I have been following the evolution of social movements since 1968, when the emancipation of social activity from the capitalist mode of production seemed possible, even imminent. This possibility has been the source of political energy for social movements from 1968 to Occupy. Throughout that period, in the Global South as well as the North, many militants and intellectuals, myself included, thought that the reproduction of capitalism was the effect of collective political will. We thought that revolutionary will could subvert and overthrow its rule.

Eventually, in the 1970s, we came to understand that capitalism is rather a *Gestalt*, a *form* that generates other forms, a tangle that contains and shapes its constituent parts. With this realization, it seemed only reasonable to abandon the expectation of revolution. Instead, we started to think in terms of autonomy: the investment in alternative possibilities for experiencing and organizing social life. Eventually we conceived of autonomy as the deployment of social potencies, but the post-industrial stage of capitalism was based on the insertion of ever more forms of social activity, particularly intellectual activity, into the logics, metrics, and infrastructures of the neoliberal financial Gestalt.

The Occupy moment marked a major, global attempt to break apart the financial command over social labor. But, among other things, the precarious fragmentation of labor made social solidarity and autonomous subjectivation hard to maintain. After the defeat of the revolutions in the Arab world and of the global Occupy movement, capital and states sought to reinforce financial rule over production and reproduction, marking a key movement in the age of extinction, an asymptotic process whose manifestation is the expanding devastation of the planet and the corruption of all forms of life. As the techno-financial machine took the upper hand, humans were pushed into a condition of political impotence. Then, impotence fueled mass humiliation and reactionary rage, pushing the social brain into a whirlwind of madness: racism, nationalism, fascism, expressions of psychopathologies that were no longer marginal or fringe.

The task of those of us interested in building autonomy is to create ever more areas of independence from the mental mayhem that is turning social energy against itself. The essays collected here aim to diagnose that chaos and present alternative forms of life.

AP One of those revolutionary actions that you underline in the book is therapy: mass therapy on a social level, which can take forms as disparate as anti-fascist organizing and collective care.

FB The revolutionary horizons of the twenty-first century are not the same as those of the twentieth. In the last century, one could envision emancipation from capitalist exploitation and a way out from the colonial oppression that most people in the world lived under. In part, this possibility was born from centuries of industrial development; in particular, new technologies made possible the drastic reduction of labor time. But as we know, this did not happen because that possibility was linked to an egalitarian culture that neoliberalism destroyed, and to a process of subjectivation based on the social composition of labor that precariousness has jeopardized. I'm certainly not the first to point out that we are working more than ever.

The word "communism" was a shorthand for expressing the revolutionary potential of the class of industrial workers in the phase marked by intense acceleration of productivity and the gradual automation of industrial labor. For political and cultural reasons, however, the communist experiment was a miserable failure, and at the end of the last century the organization of labor changed: social solidarity was seriously injured and the very concept of egalitarianism faded away. Simultaneously, the devastation of the physical environment has reached a point of irreversibility, and the acceleration of the development of the infosphere has provoked psychopathological effects that I already discussed.

The trauma produced by the Covid pandemic finally pushed people (particularly young people) into conditions of depression and impotence. The complexity of the environment (both informational and physical) has grown to a point that it can only be defined as chaos: a degree of complexity that cannot be consciously processed nor politically governed by the human mind. The outcome of this historical defeat is the spread of a wave of mental suffering that turns the world into hell. There is a question at the core of this book: is it possible to create islands of egalitarian, collective, joyous life in this hell? And my provisional answer is that it is. To get there, I propose therapy, by which I mean the political and psychoanalytical processes for creating these islands.

AP One of the major roadblocks to autonomy and to creating these islands of collective life is the development of what you call the "global automaton."

FB Well yes, but at the same time, we humans of the twenty-first century are accustomed to living inside an environment filled with and organized by automatisms, by which I mean the consequential implication of a state of being in a state of being. In other words, "If A then B" is the simplest description of an automatism, a logical and technical concatenation.

The concept of an "algorithm" instead refers to a state of being inside a *numerical* concatenation. Thanks to digital technology, algorithms are endowed with a potency of connection that turns logical automatisms into material automatisms. Financial capitalism is based on the implementation of a system in which social relations are the automated consequence of algorithms.

Furthermore, we should emphasize that there is a relation between chaos and automatisms. Chaos is an effect of acceleration: when the speed of information exceeds the capacity of mental elaboration, we are speaking of chaos. In fact, as information accelerates beyond a certain point, real processes also grow too rapid for either cognitive or political control. It's at that point that we are compelled to replace mental elaboration with technical automatisms. Thus, automatism is the effect of replacing mental decision-making with technical concatenation.

So, when artificial intelligence is inserted in the technosphere, the scattered, networked automatisms tend to merge into what I call a global automaton. Thanks to the development and introduction of self-learning software, the evolution of the global automaton grows more and more independent from the human will, which is already at pains to make sense of the chaos of the world.

AP One form of language or action that you argue can allow us to live with this chaos is poetry, precisely because it allows for recombination, reorganization, and the refusal of existing forms of power and governance. As you say in the book, "Meaningful arbitrariness is the gift that poetry offers to our minds."

FB I don't pretend to have a definition of the word "poetry," since it's a field of activity that necessarily escapes precise meaning. Rather, I envision poetry as the excess of the field of signification, as the premonition of a possible harmony inscribed in the present chaos, as a syntonizer, a factor of rhythmic integration between the living organism and the chaotic environment.

In his last book, *Chaosmosis*, Félix Guattari speaks of a sort of spasm, a painful convulsion that results from the long-lasting violence that capitalism has enacted on the social body and the social mind. This "chaosmic" spasm can be described as a rhythmic disruption or a disharmony in the relation between breathing rhythms and the rhythms of the surrounding environment. Poetry is a way to find a sort of rhythmic synchronization between our respiration and the chaotic rhythm of the environment. It is a way to overcome the sense of suffocation by finding breath.

"I can't breathe" were the words panted by Eric Garner before he was killed, strangled by a police officer on the streets of Staten Island. They are also the words that were uttered by George Floyd before he was murdered by Minneapolis police. These words perfectly describe the overall sentiment of our time.

The rebels who marched in Portland during the uprisings that followed Floyd's killing chanted the words: "Stay together, stay tight, we do it every night." This is poetry, a condition of marching together, the possibility of sharing the same rhythm, the possibility of breathing together, and also a condition for shared imagination.

AP This book speaks of the dialectical relationship between two phenomena that you have described here: the global crisis of political impotence, as you term it, and the further precarization of continually more forms of life. How do you think of the "general intellect" with this dialectic?

FB This book wants to be read as an attempt to understand the current developments of the general intellect, the collective author of technology, as they relate to the social brain. Capitalism has submitted the potency of the social brain to the rule of profit and in the process has severed the link between knowledge and social solidarity. Under the present conditions, artificial intelligence is destined to be the final enforcer of exploitation and of devastation. This much I can say is evident. Inside the framework of profit and financial accumulation, the general intellect has been turned into a termination machine.

However, I am also (and mostly) interested in what is not evident. We do not know what artificial intelligence might become if the general intellect is linked with a condition of social solidarity. I have no fear of AI itself. I fear of what AI will do when it becomes the enforcer and technical expression of the interests of profit.

The essays that I have written over the last fifteen years that are collected and edited here have attempted an analysis of the changing relation between the general intellect and capitalist power, but also an investigation of all the unknown islands of autonomy that may open the doors to liberation.

The unpredictable that can be perceived by the poetical mind is the hidden possibility of solidarity as emancipation of the general intellect from its capitalist destiny.

July 14, 2023

COGNITARIAN SUBJECTIVATION

2010

Recent years have witnessed a new techno-social framework of contemporary subjectivation. I would like to ask whether a process of autonomous, collective self-definition is possible in the present age. The concept of the "general intellect" associated with Italian post-operaist thought in the 1990s (Paolo Virno, Maurizio Lazzarato, Christian Marazzi, and others) emphasizes the interaction between labor and language: social labor is the endless recombination of myriad fragments that produce, elaborate, distribute, and decode signs and informational units of all kinds. Every semiotic segment produced by the "information worker" must meet and match innumerable other semiotic segments in order to form the combinatory frame of the info-commodity: semiocapital.

Semiocapital puts neuro-psychic energies to work, submitting them to mechanistic speed, compelling cognitive activity to follow the rhythm of networked productivity. As a result, the emotional sphere linked with cognition is stressed to its limit. Cyberspace overloads cybertime, because cyberspace is an unbounded sphere whose speed can accelerate without limits, while cybertime (the organic time of attention, memory, imagination) cannot be sped up beyond a certain point—or it cracks. And it actually is cracking, collapsing under the stress of hyper-productivity. An epidemic of panic and depression is now spreading throughout the circuits of the social brain. The current crisis in the global economy has much to do with this nervous breakdown. Marx spoke of overproduction, meaning the excess of available goods that could not be absorbed by the social market. But today it is the social brain that is assaulted by an overwhelming supply of attention-demanding goods. The social factory has become the factory of unhappiness: the assembly line of networked production is directly exploiting the emotional energy of the cognitive class.

I wish to pinpoint the problem of organic limits, which is often eclipsed by an emphasis on the limitless potential of technology. We should speak of technology in context, and the present context of technology is culturally oriented towards economic competition. Info-producers are neuro-workers. Their nervous systems act as active receiving terminals. They are sensitive to semiotic activation throughout the entire day. What emotional, psychic, existential price does the constant cognitive stress of permanent cognitive electrocution exact? The acceleration of network technologies, the general condition of precariousness, and the dependence on cognitive labor all induce pathological effects in the social mind, saturating attention time, compressing the sphere of emotion and sensitivity, as is shown by psychiatrists who have observed a steep increase in manic depression and suicide in the last generation of workers.

The colonization of time has been a fundamental issue in the modern history of capitalist development: the anthropological mutation that capitalism produced in the human mind and in daily life has, above all, transformed the perception of time. But we are now leaping into the unknown: digital technologies have enabled absolute acceleration, and the short-circuiting of attention time. As info-workers are exposed to a growing mass of stimuli that cannot be dealt with according to the intensive modalities of pleasure and knowledge, acceleration leads to an impoverishment of experience. More information, less meaning. More information, less pleasure. Sensibility is activated in time. Sensuality is slow. Deep, intense elaboration becomes impossible when the stimulus is too fast. A process of desensitization is underway at the point where electronic cyberspace intersects with organic cybertime. The prospect of individual subjectivation, and of social subjectivation, has to be reframed in this context, and a series of radical questions arise: Is it still possible to envisage a process of collective subjectivation and social solidarity? Is it still possible to imagine a "movement" in the sense of a collective process of intellectual and political transformation of reality? Is it still possible to forge social autonomy from capitalist dominance in the psycho-economic framework of semiocapitalism?

DISMANTLING THE GENERAL INTELLECT

The refusal of work—which is better defined as a refusal of the alienation and exploitation of living time—has been the main engine of innovation, of technological development and knowledge. The organic composition of capital (as a relationship between dead labor and living labor) progressively changed throughout the twentieth century as workers' resistance, their sabotage and insubordination, forced capitalists to hire engineers to replace human labor with machines. Similarly, the intellectualization of human activity is—from any perspective—a consequence of workers' insubordination and resistance to exploitation. When the cost of labor increases (as happened in the 1960s and '70s), the capitalist replaces worker with machine, as the machine is less costly in the long run. Following massive waves of industrial workers' resistance, information technology has helped to replace human toil with intelligent machines, and this has provoked the enhancement of the sphere of intellectual labor and cognitive activity linked to value production.

The '90s were a decade of alliances: cognitive labor and venture capital met and merged in the dot-com. Expectations were high, judging by the amount of investment, and creativity became an inherent feature of social labor. Then, after the dot-com bubble burst in spring 2000, neoliberalism broke the alliance of cognitive labor and venture capital. Using technology itself, neoliberalism managed to subvert the social and political *rapport de force* between labor and capital. As far as we can see now, the result of neoliberal politics is a general reduction of labor costs and an impoverishment of the cognitarians. Both industrial labor, delocalized to the peripheral areas of the world, and cognitive labor are devalued and underpaid, as precarization has fragmented and finally destroyed social solidarity. In this new context, defined by the precarization of cognitive labor, we must rethink the question of subjectivation.

Just after the financial collapse of spring 2000, the dot-com crash, and the crumbling of big corporations like Enron and WorldCom, the Swiss philosopher and economist Christian Marazzi, a sharp analyst of the social implications of financial crises, wrote an article on the danger of privatizing the general intellect, in which he predicted the trend that ten years later is in full swing: the reduction of research funding, the manipulation and militarization of state-financed research, and the impoverishment and precarization of cognitive labor.[1]

1. Christian Marazzi, "The Privatization of the General Intellect," trans. Nicolas Guilhot, https://destructural.files.wordpress.com/2010/10/christian-marazzi-the-privatization-of-the-general-intellect.pdf.

If we look at the politics of the European neoliberal ruling class, we see that they are doing exactly this: in some countries (such as Italy), they are reducing financing for schools and for research, privatizing public schools, and provoking a large-scale de-scholarization that has already begun showing signs of producing widespread ignorance and fanaticism. In some countries (like France), they increasingly limit public financing for research that cannot immediately translate into economic growth. Subjugating research to immediate economic interests reduces the role of research, rendering it a mere tool for governance, for the repetition of an existing framework of social activity. As cognitive workers are forced into precarity, they are also denied the possibility of deciding the scope of their own research. This obviously reduces the creativity invested by cognitarians in their work, as well as the pace of innovation and progress in technology.

In the long run, this trend obliterates the progressive features of capitalism. As the cost of labor becomes so low that exploiting the physical force of a worker costs less than looking for some technological replacement, the push toward innovation slows to a halt. The interest in immediate profit prevails over the long-term development of productive force. Notwithstanding the shortsighted opinions prevailing in the field of neoliberal economics, a decrease in labor costs suggests that the progressive impulse of capitalism is fading; capitalism becomes a factor of de-civilization, of intellectual and technological regression.

COGNITARIANS SEARCHING FOR A BODY

Cognitarians are those who embody the general intellect in its many forms: they process information in order to give birth to goods and services. As the cognitive function of society is inscribed in the process of capital valorization, the infinitely fragmented mosaic of cognitive activity becomes a fluid process within a universal telematic network, redefining the shape of labor and capital. Capital becomes the generalized semiotic flux that runs through the veins of the global economy, while labor becomes the constant activation of the intelligence of countless semiotic agents linked to one another.

Cognitarians are the social body of the soul at work in the sphere of semiocapital, but this body is dimidiated in a sphere isolated from the other's body. The form of alienation that is spreading in the living sphere of the cognitarians is a form of psychic suffering that escapes the Freudian definition of neurosis. If Freud's definition of neurosis lingered on the repression of desire, semiocapital is pushing demand for consumerist hyper-expression: *just do it*. Panic, depression, and a deactivation of empathy—it is here that we find the cognitariat's problem.

Precarious cognitive workers are forced to think in terms of competition. You can become friends with another person on Facebook, but genuine friendship is difficult under conditions of virtual isolation and intense economic competition. If we want to find the way towards autonomous collective subjectivation, we have to generate cognitarian awareness with regard to an erotic, social body of the general intellect. The way to autonomous and collective subjectivation starts here: from the general intellect searching for a body.

Our main political task must be handled with the conceptual tools of psychotherapy and the language of poetry—much more than the language of politics and the conceptual tools of modern political science. The political organizer of cognitarians must be able to do away with panic and depression, to speak in a way that sensibly enacts a paradigm shift, a re-semiotization of the social field, a change in social expectations and self-perception. We are forced to acknowledge that we do have a body, a social and a physical body, a socioeconomic body.

Cyber-optimists were fashionable in the '90s, and they were able to interpret the spirit of an alliance between venture capitalists and artists or engineers. But the alliance was broken during the Bush years, when technology was submitted to the laws of war, and financial capitalism provoked a collapse that may still lead to the destruction of modern civilization. Today, cyber-optimism sounds fake, like advertising for a rotten product. In his recent book, *You Are Not a Gadget*, Jaron Lanier, who engineered virtual-reality tools, writes:

> True believers in the hive mind seem to think that no number of layers of abstraction in a financial system can dull the efficacy of the system. According to the new ideology, which is a blending of cyber-cloud and neo-Milton Friedman economics, the market will not only do its best, it will do better the less people understand it. I disagree. The financial crisis brought about by the U.S. mortgage meltdown of 2008 was a case of too many people believing in the cloud too much.[2]

GOVERNANCE AND COGNITIVE SUBJUGATION

In the present, agonizing phase of neoliberalism (an agony that is more ferocious and destructive than the previous phases), European governments are staging an assault on the educational system—and particularly on scientific research—as a part of a war against cognitive labor, a war aimed at its subjugation. The university system across Europe is based on a huge amount of precarious, underpaid or unpaid labor. Researchers and students have staged protests against this trend, attempting to return the educational system to its original vocation: a place of non-dogmatic knowledge, of the public sharing of culture. Research should not be subjected to any restraining criterion of functionality, because its very function is to explore solutions that, although dysfunctional in the present paradigm, may reveal new paradigmatic landscapes. This is the role of scientific research, especially when we are facing conundrums that seem unresolvable within the capitalist paradigm.

The European ruling class aims to reduce research to a method for the governance of complexity. The ideology of governance is based on the naturalization (hypostatization, I would say in Hegelian parlance) of economic reasoning. The economy has achieved the status of a universal language, of the ultimate standard of choice, whereas economics should be just a branch of knowledge among others. The normative role that the economy has acquired is

2. Jaron Lanier, *You Are Not a Gadget* (New York: Random House, 2010), 97.

unwarranted from an epistemological point of view and devastating at the social level. If research is subjected to economic conceptualization, it is no longer research, but technical management. The so-called reform of the European educational system launched in 1999 (the year of the Bologna Charter) is aimed at the separation of applied research from the questioning of the very foundations and finalities of scientific knowledge, accompanied by the subjugation of research to standards set by economic evaluation.

The epistemic implications of this move are enormous: to submit research to the laws of economic growth obliterates the most important purpose of knowledge—what Thomas Kuhn calls its "paradigmatic" function. The ability to produce paradigm shifts in the field of knowledge and in the field of experimentation depends on the autonomy of research from established standards of evaluation. Only when research can work and discover and create concepts regardless of established social interests, can knowledge move beyond repetition and open new prospects for imagination and technology.

"Governance" is the keyword for this process. Governance produces pure functionality without meaning, the automation of thought and of will. It embeds abstract connections in the relation between living organisms, technologically subjecting choices to logical concatenation. It recombines compatible (or compatibilized) fragments of knowledge. Governance is the replacement of political will with a system of automatic technicalities that forces reality into a logical framework that cannot be questioned. Financial stability, competitiveness, labor-cost reduction, increases in productivity: the systemic architecture of EU rule is based on such dogmatic foundations that cannot be challenged or discussed, because they are embedded in the technical function of managerial subsystems. No enunciation or action is operational if it does not comply with embedded rules of techno-linguistic *dispositifs* of daily exchange.

Governance is the management of a system that is too complex to be governed. The word "government" implies the understanding (as a reduction to a rational model) of the social world, and the ability of the human will (despotic, democratic, and so forth) to control a flow of information sufficient for the control of a relevant part of the social whole. The possibility of government requires a low degree of complexity with regard to social information. Information complexity grew throughout the late modern age and exploded in the age of the digital network. Therefore, the reduction of social information to comprehensive knowledge and political control becomes an impossible task: control becomes aleatory, uncertain, almost impossible, and an increasing number of events escape the organized will.

At this point, capitalism shifts to the mode of governance. It employs an abstract concatenation of technological functions in place of the conscious processing of a flow of information. It connects asignifying segments, to use Guattari’s term, in place of dialogic elaboration. It automatically adapts in place of forming consensus, using technical language in place of shared meaning resulting from dialogue and conflict. In place of planning, it manages disruption. It assesses the compatibility of agents entering the social game in place of mediating conflicting political interests and projects. And it employs the rhetoric of systemic complexity in place of a rhetoric of historical dialectics.

LOOKING FOR AUTONOMY

As the governance model functions perfectly on its own, it destroys the social body. Conceptualizing the field of cybernetics, Norbert Wiener argued that a system exhibiting positive feedback, in response to perturbation, increases the magnitude of perturbation. In contrast, a system that responds to a perturbation in a way that reduces its effect is said to exhibit negative feedback.

A logic of positive feedback is installed in the connection between digital technology and economic financialization because this connection tends to induce technological automatisms, and psycho-automatisms too, leading to the advancement of destructive tendencies. Look at the discourse of the European political class (almost without exception): If deregulation produced the systemic collapse with which the global economy is now confronted, we need more deregulation. If lower taxation on high incomes led to a fall in demand, let's reduce high-income taxation. If hyper-exploitation resulted in the overproduction of unsold and useless cars, let's intensify car production.

Are these people insane? I don't think so. I think they are incapable of thinking in terms of the future; they are panicking, terrorized by their own impotence; they are scared. The modern bourgeoisie was a strongly territorialized class, linked to material assets; it could not exist without a relationship to territory and community. The financial class that dominates the contemporary scene has no attachment to either territory or material production, because its power and wealth are founded on the perfect abstraction of digitally multiplied finance.

And this digital-financial hyper-abstraction is liquidating the living body of the planet, and the social body. Only the social force of the general intellect can reset the machine and initiate a paradigm shift, but this presupposes the autonomy of the general intellect, the social solidarity of cognitarians. It presupposes a process of the autonomous subjectivation of collective intelligence.

EXHAUSTION AND SENILE UTOPIA:
The European Psychosphere

2010

Among many others, Jürgen Habermas and Jacques Derrida stressed the need to create institutions for unified political decisions at the level of the European Union. In the aftermath of the Greek debt crisis that started in 2009, it seems that Europhile intellectuals have gotten what they asked for. The EU entity has been subjected to a sort of political directorate that has unfortunately only served to reveal that financial interests lie at the heart of the EU's priorities. The early stage of the European tragedy has manifested itself as the political enforcement of financial domination.

Across Europe, welfare institutions have been under attack for thirty years: full employment, labor rights, social security, retirement, public schools, public transportation—all have been weakened, neglected, or destroyed. After thirty years of neoliberal obsession, we arrive at a collapse. So, what comes next? The ruling class answers coarsely: more of the same. The further reduction of public-sector salaries, the continued rise of the retirement age. No respect for society's needs or the rights of workers.

Thatcher said thirty years ago that there is no such thing as society, and today this statement comes across as a self-fulfilling prophecy. Society is in fact dissolving, leaving space for a jungle where everyone fights against one another. Following the Greek economic crisis, monetarist dogmas have been strongly reinforced, as if more poison could act as an antidote. Reducing demand will lead to recession, and the only result will be to further concentrate capital in the hands of the financial class and further impoverish the working class.

Following the Greek financial crisis, emergency law was declared: a self-proclaimed Merkel-Sarkozy-Trichet directorate imposed a deflationary policy to be forced on the various national governments of European countries. In order to rescue the financial system, this self-proclaimed directorate diverts resources from society to the banks. And in order to revive the failed philosophy of neoliberalism, social spending is cut, salaries are lowered, the retirement age is raised, and the younger working generation is precarized. Those who do not acknowledge the great necessities of competition and growth will be cut out. Those who choose to play the game will have to accept any punishment, any renunciation, any suffering demanded by the great necessity. But who said that we must be part of this?

So far, the result of the collapse of neoliberal politics has been its confirmation and consolidation. When the American financial system collapsed, there was a general expectation that capital concentration would be abandoned or at least diminished, as a redistribution of wealth seemed necessary to rescue the economy. This has not taken place. The Keynesian way has not even been explored, and Paul Krugman has been left to repeat a series of perfectly reasonable options that no one is willing to consider.

Following the crisis, American society has been robbed by big finance, and now Europe is following with its own mathematical ferocity. Is there any chance of stopping this insane race? A social explosion is possible, as it is apparent that living conditions will soon become unbearable. But precarious labor and the decomposition of social solidarity may open the way to a frightening outcome: ethnic civil war on a continental scale, and the dismantling of the Union, which would unleash the worst instincts of individual nations.

In Paris, London, Barcelona, Rome, and Athens, massive demonstrations have erupted to protest the restrictive measures, but this movement is not going to stop the catastrophic aggression against social life, because the European Union is not a democracy, but a financial dictatorship whose politics are the result of unquestioned decision-making processes.

Peaceful demonstrations will not suffice to change the course of things, and violent explosions will be too easily exploited by racists and criminals. A deep change in social perception and social lifestyle will compel a growing part of society to withdraw from the economic field, from the game of work and consumption. These people will abandon individual consumption to create new, enhanced forms of co-habitation, a village economy within the metropolis.

Unless one is seized by avarice or psychotic obsession, all a human being wants is a pleasant, possibly long life, to consume what is necessary to keep fit and make love. "Civilization" is the pompous name given to all the political or moral values that make the pursuit of this lifestyle possible. Meanwhile, financial dogma states that if we want to be part of the game played in banks and markets, we must give up a pleasant, quiet life. We must give up civilization. But why should we accept this exchange? Europe's wealth does not come from the stability of the Euro or international markets. Europe is wealthy because it has millions of intellectuals, scientists, technicians, doctors, and poets. It has millions of workers who have augmented their technical knowledge for centuries. Europe is wealthy because it has historically managed to valorize competence, and not just competition, to welcome and integrate other cultures. And, it must be said, it is also wealthy because for four centuries it has ferociously exploited the physical and human resources of other continents.

Certainly, we must give up the hyper-consumption imposed on us by large corporations, but not the traditions of humanism, the Enlightenment, and socialism—not freedom, rights, and welfare. And this is not because we are attached to old principles of the past, but because it is these principles that make it possible to live decently.

The prospect of a revolution is not open to us. The concept of revolution no longer corresponds to anything because it entails an exaggerated notion of the political will over the complexity of contemporary society. Our central goal should be a shift to a new paradigm that is not centered on growth, profit, and accumulation, but rather on the full unfolding of the power of collective intelligence.

PLATITUDES

The European tragedy has been founded on a false representation of social reality, based on assumptions that contradict daily experience, but are nevertheless delivered as absolute truth, as unquestionable dogma.

Platitude 1 Public spending must be drastically cut if European budgets are to be balanced. In fact, European states have been cutting their budgets for thirty years and are now diverting financial resources from social infrastructure towards banks and corporations. This diversion has already produced extensive damage and will produce more.

Platitude 2 The European economy must compete with the emerging economies of developing countries, and this can happen only by reducing labor costs. This means that in order to become competitive, in a strictly economic sense, European life should be impoverished. And this is what is happening: unemployment is rising, education is being privatized, and racism is spreading. Nobody has ever explained why the only criterion for evaluating wealth must be financial in nature.

Platitude 3 The European worker's productivity must be increased while salaries must be reduced. This produces an effect of low demand, deflation, and depression, but also overproduction. 40 percent of cars produced in Europe will not find buyers (thank God). So why should carmakers seek to increase the productivity of their already-hyper-exploited workers? Consumption declines because salaries shrink, but also because Europeans simply do not need any more cars.

Platitude 4 The age of retirement must be raised, as there will be too many young people and too few old people in the future. The retirement age has already been raised in every European country, and now even in France. But the rationale does not make sense. The productivity of the average European worker has increased fivefold over the past fifty years, so when the time comes, fewer young people will be able to feed more old people. But in reality, raising the retirement age has nothing to do with any social concern whatsoever. Rather, it is a trick for reducing labor costs. Capitalists would much rather pay a poor, old worker a salary than a deserved pension, and leave the young to find their own way, accepting any kind of occupation, whether precarious or simply underpaid.

No European politician dares to question these fundamental platitudes. And those who protest against these devastating measures are accused of being unable to comprehend the task at hand: to advance the deregulation that produced the present collapse. The late-neoliberal ruling class states that if deregulation produced the systemic collapse, we need more deregulation. If lower taxation on high incomes led to a fall in demand, let's lower high-income taxation. If hyper-exploitation resulted in the production of unsold and useless cars, let's intensify car production. Are these people crazy? Perhaps they are panicking, in fear of their own impotence.

AESTHETICS OF EUROPE

The aesthetics of the European Union is cold by definition. The European Union was born in the aftermath of World War II with the goal of overcoming old nationalist and ideological passions, and here lies its progressive and pragmatic nature. Lately, however, this founding anti-mythological myth seems to have been blurred, confused, forgotten. In the words of Ève Charrin: "Europe is peace, Europe is prosperity ... Granite, glass and concrete: depressing architectural neutrality ... This modesty without grace is a way of pretending that we are not political (rather, we are only managing)."[1]

Charrin expresses the aesthetic predicament of the European Union over the past decades, but such an apathetic way of being together was only possible under prosperous conditions. Insofar as a growing level of consumption could be guaranteed within the EU, monetarist rule could favor economic growth and the EU could exist as an entity. It is a fiction of democracy governed by an autocratic organism, the European Central Bank. While the US Federal Reserve was established to stabilize the value of currency and maximize employment, the primary goal of the ECB charter is to fight inflation. Now this goal has become irrational, as deflation is the overwhelming trend.

Citizens can do nothing to influence the politics of the ECB, as the Bank does not respond to political authority, and therefore European citizens have been conscious of the vacuity of European elections. In the future, these citizens will come to view the EU as their enemy.

1. Ève Charrin, "La Belgique, vertige de l'Europe," *Esprit* 353 (March–April 2009): 31–42.

Social movements should focus on the founding myth of European history: the myth of energy. Modern culture and political imagination have emphasized the virtues of youth, of passion and energy, aggression, and growth. Capitalism is based on the exploitation of physical energy, and semiocapitalism has subjugated the nervous energy of society to the point of collapse. The notion of exhaustion has always been anathema to the discourse of modernity, of Romantic Sturm und Drang, of the Faustian drive to immortality, the endless thirst for economic growth and profit, the denial of organic limits.

The Romantic cult of youth is the cultural source of nationalism. In the colonial era, British and French nationalism was the cultural condition of colonial expansion, but in the late nineteenth and early twentieth century, nationalism resurfaced to express the self-affirmation of young countries (Italy, Japan, and Germany), while the old empires (Russia, Austria, and the Ottomans) headed towards collapse. Nationalism also affirms the role of the young generation at the cultural and economic level. Old-fashioned styles are devalued, old people and women are despised for their weakness. Fascism always depicts itself as the young nation.

In late modernity, this depiction became an essential feature of advertising. But contrary to Fascist discourse, late modern advertising did not abuse old age, but denied it, claiming that every old person could be young if he or she would simply accept to partake in the consumerist feast. As Norman Spinrad showed in his novel *Bug Jack Barron* (1967), the denial of age and time marks the ultimate delirium of the global class.

We may define the old Fascism that triumphed in Italy after 1922 as a form of *energolatreia* (worshipping of energy), an expression of youth. Mussolini’s followers were young people who had survived the trauma of war and the trauma of the 1918 Spanish-flu pandemic. They reacted to the trauma by exalting the aggressive side of young exuberance. Futurism was the expression of this culture.

Berlusconi restages the same arrogance, but the actors of the present comedy are old men who require make up and Viagra to inhabit an image of energy and potency. Like the heroic mythology of Fascism, as well as the mythology of advertising embodied by

Berlusconi's subculture, the myth is based on a delirium of power. Where the former was based on the youthful virtues of strength, energy, and pride, the latter employs the mature virtues of technique, deception, and finance. And while the nemesis that followed the youthful violence of Fascism in Italy was World War II and its unthinkable mass destruction and death, one must ask what nemesis will be brought about by the present *energolatreia* of older people?

Until some decades ago, it was rare to find a person older than sixty, and while many were surrounded by an aura of respect and veneration, many others were banished to the borders of society, where they would find themselves alone, deprived of the means of survival and unable to form a community. We know very little about growing old, and we know nothing about the emotions of the elderly and their abilities for cultivating social organization, solidarity, and political force. We don't know because we have not yet experienced it. But that experience is now beginning.

The destiny of Europe will be played out in the biopolitical sphere, at the border between consumerism, techno-sanitarian youth-styled aggressiveness, and possible collective consciousness of the limits of the biological (sensitive) organism. The age of senilization is here, and Europe is the place where this experience will first find its voice.

A THERAPEUTIC PARADOX

Exhaustion has no place in Western culture, and this has become a problem, for exhaustion now needs to be understood and accepted as a new paradigm for social life. Its cultural and psychic articulation will open the door to a new conception of prosperity and happiness. The coming European insurrection will not be driven by energy, but by slowness, withdrawal, and exhaustion. It will be the autonomization of the collective body and soul from exploitation by means of speed and competition.

2. Donella H. Meadows, Dennis L. Meadows, Jørgen Randers, and William Bahrens, *The Limits to Growth* (New York: Potomac Association, 1972).

Western people were first advised of exhaustion in 1972, when the Club of Rome commissioned the book *The Limits to Growth*.[2] For the first time, we became aware that the physical resources of the planet are not boundless. Some months after the publication of the report, the Western world experienced the first oil shortage following the Yom Kippur War in 1973. Since then, we have been expected to be conscious of the fact that energy is leaving the physical body of the earth. At the beginning of the twenty-first century, the collapse of the dot-com economy led to the pauperization and precarization of cognitive workers, while the financial meltdown of September 2008 initiated a process of pauperization and precarization of society overall. Western culture is unprepared to deal with the patterns exposed by these crises, because it is a culture based on the identification of energy and good, of expansion and social well-being.

At the moment, the change in perception towards exhaustion seems rather dark and depressing, because the game is played following the rules of modern *energolatria*, a.k.a. growth. In the coming years, one third of the European population—the generation born after World War II, when the fulfillment of the modern promise of peace, democracy, and well-being was apparently at hand—will reach old age. The new generation now entering the labor market does not possess the memory of this past civilization, nor the political force to defend their existence from the predatory economy. The age of senility is here, and it may introduce a generalized form of *dementia senilis*: fear of the unknown, xenophobia, loss of historical memory. But in a different scenario—one that we should anticipate at the cultural level—the process of senilization may open the way to a cultural revolution based on the force of exhaustion, of facing the inevitable with grace, discovering the sensuous slowness of those who do not expect any more from life than wisdom—the wisdom of those who have seen a great deal without forgetting, who look at each thing as if for the first time.

This is the lesson that Europe may learn if it can come out from the capitalist obsession with accumulation, property, and greed. In a reversal of the energetic subjectivation that animated the revolutionary theories of the twentieth century, radicalism should abandon the mode of activism and adopt a passive mode. A radical passivity would dispel the ethos of relentless productivity that neoliberal politics has imposed. The mother of all the bubbles, the bubble of work, would finally deflate. We have been working too much over the past three or four centuries, and outrageously too much over the last thirty years. If a creative consciousness of exhaustion could arise, the current depression may mark the beginning of a massive abandonment of competition, consumerist drive, and dependence on work.

Gregory Bateson would define the European malaise in terms of a double bind, or contradictory injunction, with a paradoxical solution that could be this: don't be afraid of decline. Decline and de-growth imply a divestment in the midst of frenzied competition, and this is the paradox that may bring us out of the neoliberal double bind.

NIGHTMARES AND SCREENS

2012

DON'T TAKE SHELTER

In the film, *Take Shelter* (2011), the protagonist Curtis's nightmares are frightening. He dreams of a yellow-brownish rain and of a tempest destroying his wife and daughter as well as their house, one of those depressing comfortable houses scattered in the sad, flat landscape of the American Midwest. Is the nightmare to become his life or is his life already a nightmare? His life seems happy. He loves his wife Samantha and his daughter Hannah, who is hearing-impaired. Thankfully, the company he works for gives Curtis good health insurance that will cover the surgery to fix Hannah's hearing. Samantha is a stay-at-home mom. Money is tight, but thanks to his job, Curtis manages to pay the mortgage on the house.

But during the night, Curtis's sleep is troubled by premonitions of a catastrophe. He decides to build a storm shelter in his backyard. To build the shelter he needs money. His salary is not enough for the task, so he goes to the bank and asks for a loan. "Beware, my boy," says the good bank director. "These are difficult times, you have a family, running into debt is dangerous."[1] But Curtis insists. He needs money to build a shelter and protect his family from the imaginary tempest.

Significantly, director Jeff Nichols sets his movie at the end of 2008, after the Lehman Brothers breakdown. In the contemporary imagination, finance is more and more linked to catastrophic events.

Samantha is worried. Her husband's behavior has become strange. She is alarmed by the loan, and she reasons that Curtis has mental problems. She knows that his mother suffers from paranoid schizophrenia.

Then things worsen. To dig a hole for the underground shelter, Curtis takes a backhoe from the place where he works. His boss finds out, and Curtis is fired. He is now jobless, anguished, on the brink of a nervous breakdown. The shelter is ready, and one night a tornado warning sends him and his family into the shelter. They sleep in the shelter, but the tempest is not the final catastrophe. The

1. *Take Shelter*, directed by Jeff Nichols, Hydraulx Entertainment, 2011.

following morning, the sun shines brightly as their neighbors clean up the debris.

Samantha persuades Curtis to go see a therapist. The doctor suggests they take a beach vacation before Curtis begins real therapy. When they get back, he will be more relaxed and ready to start a new life. They go to the beach for a few days.

Curtis is on the beach with his daughter. They are building a sandcastle when the little girl looks at the horizon and makes the sign of a storm. Curtis turns and looks at the sky: ominous clouds are announcing the most frightening of storms. Samantha comes out of the house running, and the thick, brownish rain of Curtis's nightmares begins to fall. She looks at the ocean, where the tide is pulling back and a tsunami is growing in the distance.

Take Shelter recalls Alfred Hitchcock's *The Birds* (1963), not only in its sequences that involve birds attacking humans, but in the inexplicable premonition of an indefinable threat. The premonition gives voice to the present global unconscious, the inner landscape of mankind ravaged by financial predation and coming environmental catastrophe.

Should we take shelter? Should we go to the bank and ask for a loan, and invest in protecting our future? Should we take our premonitions seriously?

Should we accept the idea that paranoia is the proper understanding of a danger we cannot dispel?

Nichols answers our questions: investing our energy in building shelter is how we fall into the trap; it is to accept the dilemma of depression and catastrophe. When the tempest comes, we won't be home anyway. We'll be too far away from shelter.

September 11, 2012. Eleven years after the inconceivable explosion of terror, signs of a tsunami are gathering in Europe. One million people march in Barcelona under the banner of Independent Catalonia, recalling Zagreb in 1992.

No way out, and no shelter in sight. Anti-German hatred is growing in the minds of the population of Southern Europe. The European hope is turning into a nightmare, as Northern Protestants don't want to pay the bill for "lazy" Southern Catholics and Orthodox populations. Goldman Sachs has sown wind, and now the harvest is ripe for a tempest.

Money is our shelter, the only way to access life. But if you want money, you have to simultaneously renounce life. Don't build shelter, it is surely going to be useless. Furthermore, building shelters is the job of those who are preparing the storm.

Stay relaxed. Don't be attached to life, and most of all: don't have hope, that poisonous, addictive drug. Only those who are hopeless know the unspeakable way to happiness.

ITALIAN REALITY, FRONTLINE OF SEMIOCAPITAL

> For most people there are only two places in the world. Where they live and their TV set. If a thing happens on television, we have every right to find it fascinating, whatever it is.
>
> —Don DeLillo, *White Noise*, 1985[2]

Some decades ago, screens started to intrude upon urban space, the house, and daily life. First it was television, then the computer, then, everywhere in the city, huge advertising screens filled the space of our visual perception. Then, little by little—or maybe all of a sudden—we entered the screen, and we lost the way back.

The opening shot of *Reality* (2012), a movie by Matteo Garrone, is from the sky. We see Mount Vesuvius, then the city of Naples, then houses and streets, then cars, then a golden coach and coachmen dressed in Baroque style. Then we enter a garden: a wedding party and fancy ball, and people disguised as clowns, everybody taking pictures and filming with video cameras, then Enzo, the hero of the party, who has become a star because he has taken part in the reality show *Il Grande Fratello*, the Italian *Big Brother*.

Luciano (Aniello Arena) is a Neapolitan fishmonger who wants to be like Enzo. He wants to be one of the lucky people who enter the House of Big Brother. He approaches Enzo. Later, he goes to Rome

2. Don DeLillo, *White Noise* (Penguin, 2009).

for an audition. He starts to believe that he is going to be accepted, that he will enter the screen as a contestant, that he will win and gain fame and fortune for himself and his family.

He does not want to continue his normal life. He sells his fish shop, he gives away the tawdry things of his house, and he squabbles with his wife, who is conscious of the growing madness that is destroying her husband. But time passes and the TV people don't call. Little by little, Luciano falls into depression. He spends his time watching the lucky winners on TV.

At the end, totally out of his mind, Luciano goes to Rome for a religious ceremony. He finds the Big Brother house and sneaks inside. He peeks at the idiotic activities of the lucky ones who are inside the screen, and he feels that he is happy there, and lies down in a corner of the house.

Then the camera detaches itself, going away, far away, sky high. Luciano is down there, getting smaller and smaller, and at the end he disappears, a small point of light in the darkness of the night.

The fascination with the screen captures the mind, and the capture becomes irreversible, since everything happens in the space of the mind. *Reality* is the ultimate movie about contemporary power. When everybody in Italy is persuaded that Berlusconi has lost his power, Garrone tells us the truth. It's a deception. Berlusconi can be politically defeated, and some consultant from Goldman Sachs can take his place only to pursue the same politics; a center-left coalition can win the next elections, but Italy will never come out from the screen.

The movie is simultaneously very much in the neorealist style and in the surrealist Baroque style, because the Baroque is the reality of modern Italian history.

Those who think that Italy is a backward place—the corrupted side of good neoliberal postmodernity (as the Italian Left thinks)—are totally wrong. They do not understand that the reality of semiocapital is based on optical illusion and deception, on the hypertrophy of the image and the inflationary proliferation of language, on the predatory manipulation of exchange (linguistic exchange and economic exchange, mixed together and confused).

Italian absentmindedness, Italian mafia culture, and Italian political corruption are absolutely not exceptions to global neoliberal order. They are not marginal nor backward aspects of the present becoming of the world. On the contrary, the Baroque is the style of semiocapitalism, and Italy is the frontline of the global regime of financial dictatorship.

Italy has been the laboratory of power since Benito Mussolini set the Baroque of Italian Fascism (the decoration, the show, the simulation) against old Weberian bourgeois capitalism. The old, ethically motivated Protestant bourgeoisie, the class that built industrial modernity, was slowly exiting the scene of power. Italian people, who are deeply fascist because of the cultural and aesthetic history of their country, have not betrayed their mission: they have reclaimed the space of deception, of the phantasmagoria of immaterial semioproduction, whose culmination is financial abstraction.

Anti-fascist resistance during World War II was an expression of a small minority of cosmopolitan intellectuals. The decade of '68 was totally un-Italian, and the culture of Autonomia Operaia has been the only experience that smacks of cosmopolitan culture in a country that has never come out from the fascist screen.

Berlusconi, who represents the economic interests and the culture of the Sicilian-Milanese mafia, is the continuation of the Baroque style of Mussolini, finding in the TV screen its perfect framework.

In the twentieth century, Italy has been the laboratory of semiocapitalism—intimately Baroque, and intimately fascist.

PASOLINI IN TOTTENHAM

2013

I don't know if Pasolini ever visited the United Kingdom. It's not so important. Nonetheless, I would like to talk about Pasolini in Tottenham. I want to question the sensibility of the poet of Roman *borgate* from the point of view of a violent rebellion of lumpenproletarians that took place in the English suburbs in August 2011.

The visions and predictions that we find in his writings and films are good starting points for a discussion about what happened in the streets of Tottenham and Peckham, and also about what is going to happen in the coming months and years all over Europe, in the insurrection that has already started and that will continue to rage everywhere on the Old Continent—a continent that is turning into a region of violence and misery thanks to neoliberal politics, financial dictatorship, and the ignorance and dogmatism of the European ruling class.

MEETING PASOLINI

I met Pasolini in 1965, or maybe 1966, when as a schoolboy I went to see *The Gospel According to Matthew* with Professor Corrado Festi, a blind man who taught philosophy in the high school where I studied. Professor Festi was a libertarian communist who brought a student or two to the movies with him because he needed someone to explain what they were seeing, so that he himself could see. I met Pasolini again in 1968, after the Valle Giulia riots, when, for the first time in Italy, the students did not run away from the rampaging police, but instead reacted and fought back. After Valle Giulia, Pasolini wrote a poem—a bad poem in my opinion, rancorous and sour, with little irony.

But it is interesting nonetheless. The poem's title is *"Il PCI ai giovani!"* (The Italian Communist Party to the youth), but it came to be widely known by the title *"Vi odio cari student"* (I hate you, dear students), because the magazine *L'Espresso* printed it with this alternate, slanderous name. In the poem, Pasolini accuses the student demonstrators of being the power-hungry offspring of bourgeois parents, fighting against the older generation to wrest power from their hands. Simultaneously, he declares his love for the policemen, who are young sons of farmers and workers. Old populist rhetoric, I must say. *Paccottiglia* (junk), as we say in Italian.

Then I met Pasolini for the third and final time in 1973, at the house of a mutual friend, Laura Betti. I greeted that unsmiling harsh man without much sympathy. In those years, he was publishing "Letters to Gennariello" in the pages of the newspaper *Il Corriere della sera,* and the portrait he was drawing of the young Neapolitan proletarian seemed fake to me.[1] I was dealing with young proletarians from Naples and other Southern Italian cities, and their sensibilities seemed very different from Pasolini's Gennariello. The young southerners I met in the Northern Italian factories were no less old-fashioned and instinctive than Pasolini's Gennariello, but they were much sharper and more sophisticated. They were the migrant workers organizing in the factories of Milan and Turin, the driving force behind the new wave of autonomous struggles against capitalist exploitation and industrial work. They resembled the young Fiat worker described by Balestrini in his novel *Vogliamo tutto* (We Want Everything), published some years before.

Gennariello came out of an old populist mythology that didn't speak to me in the least.

WORDS AND VISIONS

When we look at Pasolini's work, when we read his novels and his poems and his countless interviews and articles, and when we watch his movies and documentaries, we sometimes feel that we are getting lost in a labyrinth of paradoxes. I have tried to make sense of his paradoxical judgments and opinions, of his idiosyncrasies, passions, and aversions. The general conclusion that I have reached is this: when he writes, when he speaks, when he ideologizes, Pasolini is essentially a reactionary and a conformist disguised as a provocateur. But when it comes to his works that use images, Pasolini is a

1. Shortly before his murder in 1975, Pasolini published a series of letters addressed to an imaginary student named Gennariello, a young boy from Naples, in the Italian newspaper *Il Corriere della sera*.

visionary, almost a prophet, and he is able to see much further than anybody else. Although a bad poet and an old-fashioned ideologue whose knowledge of Marxist philosophy was quite poor, Pasolini was a man of extraordinary vision.

In my opinion, he did not understand the meaning of the student movement of '68. It is true that many of the students who took to the streets in that year, in Italy and France and elsewhere, were probably the offspring of bourgeois parents. Many were born to professionals and the petit bourgeoisie. However, others came from working-class families, even though access to universities was still limited for the children of workers. That said, sociological considerations like these do not really get to the heart of the matter.

The meaning of the upheaval that shook the world in '68 can only be grasped by looking at the long-term recomposition of labor that took place during that period, transforming the technological structure of the production process. That movement marked the initial emergence of cognitive work, which in the following decades became the main engine of capitalist (re)production. The alliance between students and industrial workers was not a rhetorical exhibition of solidarity, but a sign of the increasing productivity and interdependence of industrial labor, the application of new technologies, and the prospect of liberating social time from the slavery of labor.

Pasolini was totally wrong in his appraisal of the student movement because he missed a crucial point: the social origin of the students was as important as the new role that cognitive work was destined to play in the transformation of capitalist production and in the political recomposition of the working class.

GENNARIELLO, TRUE AND FALSE

In the following years, however, Pasolini's relationship to the movement changed: he was pushed by the very force of events to acknowledge the proletarian character of the students, and he drew close to Lotta Continua (Continuous Struggle), a leftist organization that mixed Marxism, Maoism, and anarchism, with a generous helping of Christian radicalism. Together with Lotta Continua, Pasolini made a movie entitled *12 Dicembre*. It is not hard to understand Pasolini's attraction to Lotta Continua. "The priority of these young militants is passion and sentiment," he said. And a certain degree of theoretical inaccuracy—what we call "*pressapochismo*" (carelessness)—helped. Lotta Continua was not a political organization, but a climate of mind, a feeling which sometimes verged on populism. A broad feeling of love for the people, the destitute, and the dispossessed was the common ground of Lotta Continua and Pasolini.

In "Letters to Gennariello," this love for the poor melded with a mythology about the supposed authenticity of the young, pre-modern Neapolitan young man whom the writer wanted to protect from the contamination of consumerism and modern coarseness. But this mythology was empty and fake: the true Gennariellos in those years were not so naive and unsophisticated as Pasolini liked to imagine. In 1973, young workers from Southern Italy occupied the Fiat factory in Turin, and in 1977 they launched a general insurrection that reached its peak in Rome and Bologna in the spring of that year.

Having been killed in November 1975, Pasolini did not see the explosion of 1977. So, we cannot say whether he would have recognized the insurgents of Rome and Bologna as the brothers of his Gennariello. I don't think so. Rather, I think Pasolini would have joined the Stalinists of the Italian Communist Party (who after '89 converted to neoliberalism, but in '77 still worshipped the supreme authority of the State) in condemning the delirium and madness of Mao-Dadaists and *Indiani Metropolitani*.[2] But who knows?

FASCISM BELONGS TO THE FUTURE

While Pasolini certainly misunderstood the historical process encompassing the student upheaval, on some crucial points he was able to see (and I mean *to see*) things that we missed completely. The main mistake of the Italian student movement, and the mistake of the intellectual groups that were the progressive soul of

2. *The Indiani Metropolitani* (Metropolitan Indians) were one so-called creative wing of the Italian student movement who often dressed up in heavily caricatured costumes, mimicking Indigenous peoples from North America.

that movement—my personal mistake and the mistake of *Potere Operaio* (Workers' Power), the group I was part of—was exactly in thinking that fascism belonged to the past. We thought that the enemy of students and workers was the neo-capitalist, social-democratic bourgeoisie. Fascists still existed, of course, but we thought of them as throwbacks from the dark past of Mussolini, isolated criminals whom the ruling class could use at its convenience to scare the popular movement, to divert the attention of the workers from the struggle against capitalist exploitation.

This is why the movement launched self-defeating campaigns of *antifascismo militante* (militant antifascism) that only managed to fall into the trap of violence—hammering at some black-clad idiots and being hammered by them. We were dead wrong, because fascism is not something that belongs to the past. Fascism belongs to the future. This is what Pasolini clearly saw, although he was unable to explain it in plain theoretical words. Pasolini rightly linked fascism to sexual humiliation, consumerism, ignorance, rage, and ugliness. All of these have been on the rise during the years of neoliberal dictatorship. Ugliness is everywhere—in cities ravaged by speculation, in bodies wasted by exploitation and loneliness, on ubiquitous advertising billboards and television screens.

It is not easy to say what fascism means. Humbly, I might propose that fascism is a pathology of identity: a pathology hitting those who are too weak to accept the idea that identity is ever-changing and multifarious, and too frightened by their own uncertainty and ambivalence. Pasolini was able to predict the spread of this ambivalence, this fear, this frailty, and to foresee the epidemic of rage that was destined to emerge from it.

PASOLINI IN TOTTENHAM

Now I come to Tottenham. A young man, Mark Duggan, was killed in Tottenham by police on August 4, 2011. After his death, thousands of young workers, unemployed people, and students took to the streets in the suburbs of London, Birmingham, and Manchester, and attacked banks and shops, stealing goods from supermarkets, setting houses ablaze, and attacking the police. The British Prime Minister, quickly called back from his holiday in Tuscany, declared that they were common criminals.

I try to look at the four nights of rage from Pasolini's point of view. Fascist consumerism, or lumpen desacralization of consumerist rituals? Personally, I despise the priggish journalists and hypocritical intellectuals who screamed in Murdoch's newspapers that the riots were not political events, but coarse acts of consumerist violence. During the last thirty years or so, media, advertising, and neoliberal idealogues have obsessively repeated a message to young people: life is competition, and the field of competition is consumption. The more gadgets you have, the better your life will be, even if you have to endure exploitation and humiliation every day. Now, all of a sudden, the kids have been told that they have to pay the debt accumulated by the financial class. Social spending must be cut and there will be no jobs for young people. It is no wonder that people who have been promised lots of gadgets in exchange for their lives want those gadgets at any cost.

Often in Pasolini's novels and movies, the young male body is an object of worship and contempt. Beyond its sexual undertones, this ambivalence has a political and cultural meaning: the beautiful and the criminal are joined in the same person. Think of the title character from Pasolini's film *Accattone*, simultaneously innocent and sordid.

Many say that the London rioters are just consumerist and violent. They forget that these young people have been shaped by an ugly human landscape, itself produced through thirty years of competition and consumerism. Empathy has become frail; solidarity has been ridiculed and destroyed. The rioters of London have been cultivated by Murdoch's popular magazines and TV garbage.

We should not worship this rebellion, and we should not condemn it. We should be able to accept and understand its historical meaning: capitalism is morally and economically bankrupt. From within the much-needed insurrection of the precarious generation, we should be able to create a new consciousness, a new self-perception based on solidarity, on the refusal of exploitation, on frugality, and on a culture of sharing: sharing production in the web-based world and sharing consumption in the city.

EUROPEAN INSURRECTION

Leftist intellectuals may despise consumerism and ersatz culture, but, in my view, this is not a time for moralizing. It is a time to imagine a possible social recomposition of the precarious body and of the general intellect. Cognitive labor and precariousness are not separate realities. Cognitive workers are unemployed, and precarious workers are often highly educated young people whose intellectual skills are ominously underused. Cognitarians and lumpens intermingle in daily life, and sometimes they decide to go looting together.

From looting we must move towards the liberation of the general intellect. I don't think that all the young people who took to the streets of England on those August nights were motivated by political solidarity. I believe they were motivated by many different feelings: rage, in some cases by egoistic consumerist craving, but also, in many cases, by a desire for togetherness. Insurrections are never the effect of a well-conceived project, of well-mannered intentions. Generally, insurrections start from a mix of different impulses. What matters is the ability of a minority (call them the political avant-garde, call them organic intellectuals, maybe call them schizoanalysts) to find concepts, words, and gestures that give different people a common vision and a common understanding of the real and the possible.

In the coming months, we won't need a political party. Rather, we'll need a bunch of curators for the European insurrection. We don't have to provoke the insurrection, as the insurrection is being provoked by the European Central Bank and by the cowardice and ignorance of the European ruling class. Instead, we must introduce into the unavoidable insurrection some perception of the potency of collective intelligence, and we have to connect this perception to a desire for sociality. The general intellect is looking for the erotic and social body that it lost in the process of virtualization. Similarly, precarious life is looking for a collective intelligence that is fragmented and dispersed.

In trying to imagine Pasolini on the stage of the present European insurrection, I think that he would quote Matthew's Gospel:

> Therefore I tell you, do not be anxious about your life,
> what you shall eat or what you shall drink,
> nor about your body, what you shall put on.
> Is not life more than food, and the body more than clothing?
> Look at the birds of the air: they neither sow nor reap nor gather into barns, and yet your heavenly Father feeds them.
> Are you not of more value than they?
> And which of you by being anxious can add one cubit to his span of life?
> And why are you anxious about clothing?
> Consider the lilies of the field, how they grow; they neither toil nor spin;
> yet I tell you, even Solomon in all his glory was not arrayed like one of these.
> But if God so clothes the grass of the field, which today is alive and tomorrow is thrown into the oven, will he not much more clothe you, O men of little faith?
> Therefore do not be anxious, saying, "What shall we eat?" or "What shall we drink?" or "What shall we wear?" For the Gentiles seek all these things; and our heavenly Father knows that you need them all.
> But seek first his kingdom and his righteousness, and all these things shall be yours as well. Therefore do not be anxious about tomorrow, for tomorrow will be anxious for itself. Let the day's own trouble be sufficient for the day.

I am an atheist, but I know the infinite potency of the general intellect, when it is governed by solidarity and affection, desire free of greed. We can rely on collective intelligence: it is our Father, who is on earth. It is our autonomy from any subjection, from capitalism, the state, from God.

ACCELERATIONISM QUESTIONED FROM THE POINT OF VIEW OF THE BODY

2013

Is acceleration the necessary condition for the final collapse of power?

Acceleration is an essential feature of capitalist growth: increases to productivity imply an intensification in the rhythm of exploitation. The accelerationist hypothesis, nevertheless, points out the contradictory implications of the process of intensification, emphasizing the instability that acceleration brings into the capitalist system. Contra this hypothesis, however, my answer to the question of whether acceleration marks a final collapse of power is quite simply "no." Because the power of capital is not based on stability. Naomi Klein has explained capitalism's ability to profit from catastrophe. Furthermore, capitalist power, in the age of complexity, is not based on slow, rational, conscious decisions, but on embedded automatisms, which do not move at the speed of the human brain. Rather, they move at the speed of the catastrophic process itself.

But the accelerationist hypothesis can be read from a different—more interesting—angle, as a particular version of the radical immanence in the philosophical dimension of contemporary Spinozian communist thought.

I can refer to Hardt and Negri's books. For them, the transition beyond the sphere of capitalist domination is conceived in terms of a full deployment of the tendencies implied in the present forms of production and life. Acceleration in this framework can be viewed as the full implementation of those tendencies that lead to the deployment of the inner potencies contained in the present form of capitalism.

In *Empire*, Hardt and Negri reject the deceptive pretense of an anti-globalist return to national sovereignty, and they remark on the analogy between the globalizing empire of post-national politics and the potency of the internet, which can be viewed as the realization of the potency of the general intellect.[1]

We can also find this rejection of any nostalgia for the slowness of a pre-capitalist past in the work of Deleuze and Guattari. In *Anti-Oedipus*, the rejection assumes the schizoid perspective: the schizoid is the accelerating pace of the Unconscious. Schizophrenia

1. Pope Francis, *Misercordiae Vultus*, April 11, 2015.

is all about speed: the speed of the surrounding universe in relation to the speed of mental interpretation. Yet there is no dimension of mental normalcy to restore, and, in *Anti-Oedipus*, schizophrenia is both the metaphor of capitalism and the methodology of revolutionary action:

> But which is the revolutionary path? Is there one?—To withdraw from the world market, as Samir Amin advises Third World countries to do, in a curious revival of the fascist "economic solution"? Or might it be to go in the opposite direction? To go still further, that is, in the movement of the market, of decoding and deterritorialization? For perhaps the flows are not yet deterritorialized enough, not decoded enough, from the viewpoint of a theory and a practice of a highly schizophrenic character. Not to withdraw from the process, but to go further, to "accelerate the process," as Nietzsche put it: in this matter, the truth is that we haven't seen anything yet.[2]

A popular '68 slogan proclaimed: "*Cours camarade, le vieux monde est derrière toi!*" (run comrade, the old world is behind you!). But the evolution of Deleuze and Guattari's thought shows a displacement of this point of view. In the last chapter of *What is Philosophy?*, a book they wrote twenty years after *Anti-Oedipus*, we read the following:

> We require just a little order to protect us from chaos. Nothing is more distressing than a thought that escapes itself, than ideas that fly off, that disappear hardly formed, already eroded by forgetfulness or precipitated into others that we no longer master.[3]

2. Pope Francis, interview with Antonio Spadaro, "Intervista a Papa Francesco," *La Civiltà Cattolica*, September 19, 2013.
3. Federico Campagna, "Pope Franciscus Under a Bright Red Star," *The White Review* 13 (March 2015).

What happened between the two books? Is it that the authors aged, their bodies weakening and their brains becoming slower? Maybe, but this isn't where the answer lies. The answer lies in the passage from 1972 to 1992. During this period, economic globalization and the info-technological revolution intensified the effects of acceleration on the desiring body.

The final chapter of *What is Philosophy?* concerns the crucial relation between chaos and the brain, and this is the best point of view from which to understand the effects of the accelerating machine on social subjectivity.

The reciprocal implication of desire and capitalist development can be properly understood through the concept of schizo-deterritorialization. But when it comes to the process of the recomposition of subjectivity and the formation of social solidarity, acceleration implies the submission of the Unconscious to the globalized machine. If we investigate acceleration from the point of view of sensibility and the desiring body, we see that chaos is the painful perception of speed, and acceleration is the chaotic factor leading to the spasm that Guattari speaks about in *Chaosmosis*.

Acceleration is one of the features of capitalist subjugation. The Unconscious is submitted to the ever-increasing pace of the infosphere, and this form of subsumption is painful—it generates panic before finally destroying any possible form of autonomous subjectivation.

IMMANENCE/POSSIBILITY

The dialectical (eschatological) vision of communism as the final realization of a superior form of society following the abolition of capitalism is the political-totalitarian translation of the Hegelian utopia of *Aufhebung*.

A materialist critique of capitalism is based on the notion that there is no transcendent dimension, and that the historical process has nothing to do with the implementation of an Ideal. The possibilities of the future are contained in the present composition of society. The possibility of a new social form is incorporated into the social relations, the technical potency, and the cultural forms that capitalism has developed. There is no outside.

We may call this conception—opposed as it is to the idealistic vision of Hegelian dialectics, which was in turn adopted by Marxist-Leninist ideology—"immanentism." It marks the difference between, on the one hand, the post-Hegelian brand of critical thought that flourished in Italian operaismo (workerism) of the 1960s and '70s, and, on the other hand, French poststructuralism.

Not surprisingly, this kind of radical materialism comes with a special celebration of Spinoza. Both Deleuze and Negri, in fact, have emphasized Spinoza's rejection of transcendentality: God is here, God is everywhere, God is Nature. We just need to see His presence and to act in a way that allows His infinite potency to emerge.

The radical materialist thinking that illuminated the path of the autonomia movement in the last decades of the twentieth century is essentially the assertion of the immanent force contained in the present social composition and which needs to be disentangled in order to deploy the potentiality of the general intellect beyond the limits of capitalism. This force is not hidden in the mind of a distinct God nor in the ideas of philosophers. It is hidden inside the present form of social production. No external force or external project can propel the process of transformation that leads to a new form of social organization, because there is no exteriority. The permanent conflict and cooperation between work and capital is the sphere in which the process of deployment happens. This is a common point in Deleuzo-Guattarian rhizomatics and in the multitudinous Spinozism of Hardt and Negri.

Not surprisingly, the reference to Marx's "Fragment on Machines" (from the *Grundrisse*) is crucial to this point of view. In that text, Marx asserts the possibility that communism is contained in the folds of the capitalist present, as a tendency embedded in the technological development of the current organization of work and knowledge. Everything is already here: the potency of the general intellect, the constant intensification of productivity, the tendency towards the emancipation of time from labor.

The tendency implied in the technological organization of capitalism leads to a new concatenation of knowledge and machines.

This immanent conception of communism has something to do with the accelerationist hypothesis, but the philosophical danger that I see in such an immanentist stance consists in mistaking the deployment of the potentiality embedded in the present composition of work and technology for a necessity.

THE ACCELERATIONIST HYPOTHESIS

The accelerationist hypothesis is based on two main points: the first is the assumption that accelerating production cycles make capitalism unstable; the second is the assumption that the potentialities contained in the capitalist form are *necessarily* going to deploy themselves.

The first assumption is belied by the experience of our time: capitalism is resilient because it does not need rational government, only automatic governance, and because it has no desiring body, being an abstract system of automatisms. Governance is exactly this: the replacement of rational government with the mere concatenation of techno-linguistic automatisms. Furthermore, acceleration is destroying social subjectivity, as the latter is based on the rhythm of bodily desire, which cannot be accelerated beyond the point of spasm.

The second assumption totally underestimates the obstacles and limitations that hinder and pervert the process of subjectivation. The immanence of the liberating form (the immanence of the autonomous deployment of the general intellect) implies the *possibility* of this deployment, but it does not imply the necessity of it. The potency of the general intellect embodied in networked production is subjected to the power of the financial matrix.

The rhizomatic theory is a methodology for the description of capitalist deterritorialization and an attempt to redefine the ground of deterritorialized subjectivation. But it is not (and it cannot be) a theory of autonomy. At many points in their work, Hardt and Negri seem to equivocate between the two: they actually promote the expectation that the social potency of the common—the general intellect—is intrinsically ordained to fully deploy itself and that capitalism is intrinsically ordained to culminate in communism. But they do not consider the possibility of a stoppage in the process of deployment, of an entanglement blocking the possible.

Their radical materialism implies the immanent nature of the possibility, but this immanence of the possibility does not equal a logical necessity. Nor does it imply the unstoppable deployment of the richness implied in the present. This possibility, indeed, can be hindered and diverted by the cultural and psychological forms of subjective existence.

The accelerationist stance, in my opinion, is an extreme manifestation of the immanentist conception. Paradoxically, it also seems to be a particular interpretation of the Baudrillardian assertion that "the only strategy now is a catastrophic strategy." The train of hypercapitalism cannot be stopped; it is going faster and faster, and we can no longer run at the same pace. The only strategy, therefore, is based on the expectation that the train is going to crash at some point, and the capitalist trajectory is going to lead to the subversion of its own inner dynamics. This is an interesting proposition to consider, but it is ultimately untrue, because the process of autonomous subjectivation is jeopardized by chaotic acceleration, and social subjectivity is captured and subjugated by capitalist governance, which is a system of automatic mechanisms running at blinding speed.

THE NEUROPLASTIC DILEMMA:
Consciousness and Evolution

2014

SUBJECTIVITY AND AUTOMATION

The history of the last fifty years can be read from the point of view of the relation between subjectivity and automation, the replacement of a living process by a technological artifact whose performances replicate the logical and functional succession of human acts. In the history of capitalism, this replacement has a double goal: increasing workers' productivity and subduing the political force of organized workers.

In the last decades of the twentieth century, the digital network became the engine for the increase of productivity in every branch of social production. The worldwide movement of students that culminated in the year 1968 can be viewed as the moment of anticipation and early emergence of this new social potency: students are the living embodiment of the general intellect, and the antiauthoritarian movements were the beginning of a long-lasting conflict between cognitive workers and capital.

The process of automation has not only replaced physical acts of production; rather, following the introduction of information technology, automation has massively transformed cognitive activity itself. The capture and subsumption of cognitive activity is the basic condition of semiocapitalism, which is based on the valorization and accumulation of signs (semia) as economic assets. In order to capture cognitive activity (attention, memory, language, imagination), semiocapital must insert automatic procedures into the field of cognition itself. Therefore, automation is not only the effect of the cognitive action that leads to the change of work organization; it also implies the reduction of cognitive activity to algorithmic procedures and the insertion of automatisms into the social existence of the general intellect.

This process poses a major threat to the autonomy of subjectivation: language, memory, and imagination are more and more performed by machines, and the human learning process is more and more pervaded by the automated process of enunciation.

DETERMINISM

Determinism is a philosophical theory based on the assumption that every physical event can be reduced to a chain of causation. In the last century, the determinist vision has simultaneously gained and lost ground. It has gained ground thanks to the refinement of tools for microphysical investigation and the discovery of highly complicated patterns of causation and determination in the field of biogenomics. But it has lost ground both in physics and in biology since Heisenberg's uncertainty principle blurred the link between physical phenomena and the observer.

In the 1990s, the Human Genome Project was founded on the assumption that genes determine an organism's life, just as code determines a message's interpretation. After the mapping of the genome, however, scientists and philosophers dispelled the determinist implications of biogenetic mapping by stressing the importance of epigenesis in the formation of living organisms. Epigenesis, in fact, is the aleatory and unpredictable effect that environment exerts on the unfolding of the bioinfo "code," transiting from zero-dimensional information to the multi-dimensional body.

According to the theory of epigenesis, the code is indeed only the palette (or the range of possibility) on which the process of generation takes place, choosing one possibility among many. The living organism does not have to be seen as the predictable unfolding of information contained within the code. It should rather be seen as the result of a sort of infinitely complex negotiation between the code and the environment, between the possibilities contained in the code and the outcome of epigenetic deployment. Epigenesis is the vibratory oscillation of a genetic flow of information that meets the environment and changes direction and shape according to environmental events.

Epigenetic theory reveals the flaw to determinism: based on the assumption that phenomena result from the predictable deployment of a coded process of generation, determinism misses the aleatory process of vibration that leads to the implementation of one possibility among many. This is why, at the end of the day, determinism has to be abandoned as a methodology for the description of reality. But determinism is not only a description; it is also a project, and, from this point of view, we have to look at it in a new way. Indeed, determinism may be viewed as a strategy based on the insertion of deterministic tools into the living organism and its brain. Cognitive automation is the technology for injecting determinism into the human sphere.

COGNITIVE AUTOMATION

The automation of cognitive activity is going to be a major trend in the coming decades, marking a leap to a post-historical dimension. In the modern humanist sense, "history" is the process of the conscious affirmation of free projects in the field of political action. But the cognitive mutation that we are talking about is going to dissolve the historical relation between consciousness, politics, and freedom. Automation is taking the place of political decision, and the word "governance" essentially refers to this automation of data interpretation and decision: it implies the end of politics, democracy, and conscious decision-making, and of the establishment of an automatic chain of logical procedures intended to replace conscious voluntary choices.

As some theorists have argued (e.g., Kevin Kelly in *Out of Control: The New Biology of Machines, Social Systems, and the Economic World*), the social organism is going to be transformed into a swarm, a collective organism composed of many individual bodies whose brains follow rules that are embedded in the nervous system of each individual.[1] The individuals who comprise a swarm act in a coordinated way, even if no centralized structure of control dictates how they should behave. Cognitive automatisms act as embedded rules, which lead to the emergence of a form of intelligent behavior that is not consciously performed by the individuals who take part in the swarm.

1. Kevin Kelly, *Out of Control: The New Biology of Machines, Social Systems, and the Economic World* (New York: Basic Books, 1995).

Under the present conditions of hypercomplexity—the excessive intensity and speed of the info-stimuli affecting the brain—social action is less and less the result of consciously organized choices, and more and more the result of automated chains of cognitive elaboration and social interaction.

Amidst the contemporary transformation of the human via the digital manipulation of language and life, human action is returning to a sort of theological dependence. Technolinguistic automatisms act like a posthumanist God, whose operational force is inscrutable and superior to human action and will.

Not surprisingly, the neohuman emerges most notably from the American cultural sphere. Since the beginning of colonization, North American civilization has been marked by the erasure of cultural pasts. The cultural and religious legacy of the European past was canceled by the Puritans' decision to abandon the old continent, polluted as it was by religious and political corruption. The elimination of the Indigenous population (the most successful genocide ever) cleared the American setting of traces of local culture. In that territory, purified of the past, the Puritans built a new civilization which was essentially based on a verbal relationship with God.

Yes or *no*: this is the Puritan language. No nuances, no ambiguity. (Not coincidentally, it is similar to the computational language of *zero* or *one*.) In their relation to God, Puritans did not rely on images, on impure, ill-defined representations. Only words made the relation between God and the elected people possible.

Catholics invaded the Mexican cultural sphere with a flow of imagery. They founded the process of evangelization on the ambiguity of images whose interpretation is infinite and always open to semantic negotiation. The Anglo-Saxon Puritans, by contrast, laid the foundations of a binary infosphere with no ambiguity. This is the epistemic and aesthetic condition of the neohuman civilization that led Western culture to create computing technology and the digital infosphere. The next step is the utopia of the final automation of intelligent life.

TRANSHUMANISM

According to the transhumanist vision, the reduction of every process to the informational binary will give way to the emergence of a living and conscious artifact perfectly replicating human behavior. The transhuman vision can be seen as the ideological foundation of the determinist strategy. The transhuman project is based on the automation of cognitive activity and on the uploading of this automated cognitive ability to an artifact. Only by assuming that conscious behavior is the effect of a deterministic chain of causation is it possible to imagine the implementation of a technical automaton acting as a perfect replica of the human being: the android.

Not surprisingly, Ray Kurzweil—the philosopher and technofuturist who wrote the book *The Singularity Is Near*, which proposes the concept of transhumanism—was hired by Google in 2012. He is now the director of a program called "Google Brain" that involves machine learning and language processing. The inscription of determinist automatisms into cognitive activity, and the consequent inscription of determinist chains into the social sphere, is the core of the Google Empire: the capture of user attention and the translation of cognitive acts into automatic sequences. The inscription of these sequences into the sphere of language and cognition at large—this is the Google methodology, based on the replacement of cognition with a chain of automated connections, aiming at the systematic fabrication of automated subjectivity.

This project implies the insertion of deterministic chains into the epigenetic process. The transhumanist project aims to narrow the space of epigenesis and to submit epigenetic events to the determination of algorithmic chains inscribed into the body and mind. But the transhumanist project is based on a flawed idea of the human experience. Can experience be automated and reduced to chains of predictable steps? Yes and no.

Cognitive activity can be reduced to formal procedures, and these procedures can be translated into algorithms so that cognition can be replicated by an artifact and so that experience can be made uniform. But the human agent cannot be reduced to only their behavior and cognitive performances.

Cognition and life can be simulated by intelligent automata, but the replica is not identifiable with the conscious and sensible organism, because cognition and life are not reducible to the embedding of information into an artifact. As highly complex and refined as it may be, the construct can develop intelligent behavior, but not experience. Experience means the self-reflective deployment of consciousness in the temporal dimension. Experience (*ex-perire*) implies time; it implies an awareness of the temporal limit inscribed in the organism: death. There is no self if there is no consciousness of being in the flow of time. The conscious organism, indeed, is not placed in the flow of time (as if time were an external dimension that the conscious organism was going through), but is the flow of time itself. Consciousness is the experience of time and the projection of time, and no artifact can embody this experience or this consciousness. We can envision the possibility of replacing direct experience of the world with a download of recorded information, but this download cannot be called "experience."

This is the philosophical flaw of transhumanist theory. Nevertheless, transhumanist ideology and the development of automation technology are producing mutations in the conscious organism and the social body. Transhumanist theory should not be seen as a description, but rather as a project and a strategy for the reprogramming of the human brain.

THE NEUROPLASTIC DILEMMA

In 2013, President Barack Obama declared that the main scientific investment of the US in the second decade of the twenty-first century would be the Brain Activity Map (BAM) Project, a continuation of the Human Genome Project. These projects are essentially aimed at mapping the infinite possible combinations of genetic information and neural connections. Simultaneously, they raise urgent philosophical issues: the question of determinism versus indeterminism is being restated in the fields of biomorphogenesis, neuromorphogenesis, and the generation of events at large.

The emerging concept of neuroplasticity is crucial here: the transformation of the physical conditions in which cognition operates is affecting not only psychocognitive activity, but also its neurological substratum.

In her book *The New Wounded*, Catherine Malabou remarks that Freud's move from the sphere of neurology to the sphere of language and sexuality should be reversed today.[2] If we want to explain increasingly prevalent diseases like Alzheimer's and Parkinson's—afflictions that result from the degradation of the material consistency of the brain—we must go back to a neurological approach. The same can be said about a wide range of new pathologies, particularly those affecting young people who have been exposed to digital flows of info-stimulation since early childhood.

The philosophical and political implications of plasticity are ambiguous. Like the concept of determinism, the concept of neuroplasticity is double-edged: it is a description of the neural system as essentially plastic, but it is also a condition for carrying out a strategy. If the neural system is plastic, it is possible to develop a project of neurosubjection and cognitive mutation: the Google strategy. Or, conversely, if the neural system is plastic, it is possible to develop a project of neuro-emancipation from the surrounding reality.

A dilemma casts a shadow over the near future: Do we adapt our neural systems to a social and physical environment that is becoming more and more intolerable to human sensibilities? Or do we pursue the autonomous reorganization of the general intellect? The first case is already largely on display in present social behavior: thanks to the globalized media system, we are daily exposed to images of unspeakable violence, torture, humiliation, misery, and displacement, including the deportation of millions of children, women, and elderly people. But we are becoming more and more

2. Catherine Malabou, *The New Wounded: From Neurosis to Brain Damage* (New York: Fordham University Press, 2012).

capable of deactivating compassion, up to the point that mass cynicism acts like a moral anesthesia. Permanent exposure to horror deactivates our ethical sentiment. Empathy is atrophied.

But neuroplasticity can go in the opposite direction. The plasticity of our neural systems can be the condition for a fundamental reactivation of the psycho-cognitive apparatus in its social expression. Neuroplasticity can be the condition for the reactivation of empathy and political solidarity—necessary conditions for a process of self-organization of the general intellect that is driven by ethical and aesthetic sensibilities rather than by the an-ethical impulse of economic competition.

NEURO-ENGINEERING: CONSCIOUSNESS AND EVOLUTION

The unbridgeable gap between information (zero-dimensional and atemporal) and the body (multidimensional and evolving in time) is the condition of the interminability of the process of subsumption. The game is over, but the game is continually starting up again.

The current theoretical focus on neuroplasticity can pave the brain to adapt to an environment that grows every day more intolerable for a psychological, aesthetic, and ethical mind that was forged in a previous age of human civilization. Adaptation to the connective mode of communication, adaptation to the ferocity of competition, to the barbarity and horror of the submission of life and attention to financial abstraction, may take the form of a sort of social lobotomy: a pharmacological or surgical cancelation of what in the human psyche is incompatible with abstract domination.

But there is an alternative possibility. It lies in the conscious ability of the brain to reshape itself. In order to conceptualize the shift from the past forms of political action—now devoid of effectiveness—to the evolutionary horizon of conscious neuro-evolution, preliminary questions must be addressed: What is the relationship between consciousness and evolution? Can we envisage a non-deterministic adaptation to neuroplastic evolution? Can we consciously govern this neuro-evolution?

In order to answer these questions, we should focus on the relationship between aesthetic sensibility and the epistemic foundation of social action. Then we should focus on the creation of a platform (social, cultural, institutional, artistic, neuro-engineering) for the self-organization of the general intellect and the recomposition of the networked activity of millions of cognitive workers worldwide, who must be reacquainted with their social, erotic, and poetic body.

We must walk this territory where technology meets epistemology, psychopathology meets poetry, and neurobiology meets cultural evolution.

THE MESSAGE OF FRANCIS

2015

The Italian director Nanni Moretti's film *Habemus Papam* (his best, in my opinion) portrays the impotence of human beings as they face the immensity of historical suffering. God is nowhere to be found, while the newly elected Pope, played by Michel Piccoli, finds himself unable to verbally express the unimaginable chaos of reality in the absence of God.

Moretti's genius here is to have foretold a drama that actually unfolded in the Church of Rome just a few months after the film's release. In February 2013, Joseph Ratzinger, the German Pope who asserted the unquestionable superiority of truth against any relativism, decided to resign from his position, declaring physical and spiritual feebleness. This was an act of unprecedented courage and humility that we should interpret in philosophical terms as an acknowledgment of the political impotence of ethical reason.

I'm not a theologian, and I don't pretend to understand deeply the meaning and intentions behind such an enormous act. However, from the point of view of secular philosophy, I claim that the resignation of Ratzinger, or Pope Benedict XVI, marked the failure of the historical attempt to master and subdue the unchained forces of evil materialized by the animal instincts of global capitalism. Overwhelmed by his own weakness, Benedict fell silent and lowered his head. In my view, admitting his impotence was the highest sign of his fortitude.

Then something else happened. In a time when sectarian violence, conservative arrogance, and economic greed have taken the upper hand almost everywhere, a man appeared in the window of Saint Peter's Basilica and hailed the crowds of the world, simply saying: "good evening."

I'm not a believer, and my atheism makes it difficult for me to accept the idea that the Holy Spirit enlightened the high clergy who met in the papal conclave in the days of March 2013. However, human wisdom led them to elect a new pope, Francis, who seems to stand—alone—in the Church against ethnic violence, political oppression, and economic exploitation.

On April 11, 2015, Francis released his *Misericordiae Vultus* to inaugurate a Holy Year of Mercy. The document is an explicit redefinition of the relation between truth and compassion, insisting upon the superiority of compassion over truth.[1] We may replace the word "compassion" with the word "empathy," and equally so with the word "solidarity."

In an interview with Father Antonio Spadaro published by *La Civiltà Cattolica*, the Pope, who, in his own words, came from the end of the world, declares that the Church should be seen as a military field hospital:

> What the Church needs more today is the ability to heal the wounds, and to warm the heart of the believers, the proximity. I see the Church as a military field hospital. It's useless to ask a seriously wounded person if he has cholesterol. His wounds have to be healed. Then we'll speak about other things. Healing wounds is our mission ... and we must start from below.[2]

What is striking in these words is the Pope's intellectual courage to abandon the discourse of hope. In doing so, he interprets the prevailing sentiment of our time: the hopeless perception of the future. However, he translates this hopelessness in terms of mercy, compassion, and friendship.

In Christian parlance, without faith, hope is impossible. And faith seems to be over, since communism, democracy, and progressive dialectics crumbled at the end of the last century. Only capitalism survives. But faith in capitalism has collapsed as well, during the years of financial arrogance and precarious work. In the 1990s, capitalism was proclaimed to be the universal and ultimate model of social life, conquering the mind of many deficient left-wing intellectuals. Now, only twenty years later, capitalism has lost almost all of its credibility and is ruling as an unstoppable automatic machine. It is no longer winning by the force of consent; it is just subjugating souls and bodies by force.

1. Pope Francis, *Misercordiae Vultus*, April 11, 2015.
2. Pope Francis, interview with Antonio Spadaro, "Intervista a Papa Francesco," *La Civiltà Cattolica*, September 19, 2013.

I'm not a believer; I trust in no god and no ideology, so I don't think that the end of faith is a bad thing. On the contrary, I think that when we are freed from faith, we can grasp the real tendency of the time and seize the most interesting opportunities that the tendency brings about. But in order to seize the possible and actualize it, we need friendship, solidarity, happiness, and pleasure in the relations among bodies. This is what we lack today. Not hope, not faith, but friendship. This is why mankind is teetering on the abyss of war and suicide.

My interpretation of the words of Francis may be read as blasphemous, but not as incongruous with their intended meaning: God is not here to take care of our wars, pollution, or the exploitation and precariousness of work. He is possibly busy with something more urgent—who knows. Anyway, we have to do without his help. Consequently, we must abandon hope: the world machine is ungovernable, and human will is impotent. Only friendship is left. This is how I understand Francis's words.

In a fascinating text titled "Pope Franciscus Under a Bright Red Star," Federico Campagna compares the actions of the pope elected in 2013 with the actions of the pope elected in 1503: Julius II, the "'Pope dressed in armour,' the warrior Pontifex who had spent his life fighting to 'push back the barbarians.'"[3]

Campagna proposes a political interpretation of the message of Francis, the pope who summons anti-globalization and social activists, aiming to become the reference point of that part of the world population that has had no political representation on the global stage since the fall of the Communist Revolution.

As for me, I do not deny that Pope Francis's preaching has political intentions and political effects, but I don't think this is the most important message of the man. The most important, in my humble opinion, is the suggestion that Christ did not come to earth to impose justice, but to preach friendship and compassion—like Siddhartha Gautama, by the way, who similarly spoke of great compassion as the only way to harmonize the singularity of existence and the cosmic game.

3. Federico Campagna, "Pope Franciscus Under a Bright Red Star," *The White Review* 13 (March 2015).

On September 10, 1978, a pope named Albino Luciani declared that "God is more a mother than a father." He died only a few weeks after this scandalous affirmation. By saying that Christ is merciful love more than the severity of truth, Pope Francis is rephrasing Luciani's concept. With his emphasis on mercy, he suggests God's motherly attention to the frailty of the human creature, in opposition to a fatherly obsession with the Law.

Obviously, we must read this emphasis in political terms: Christians are murdered in many countries because of their religious belonging. But Francis is not calling for a Crusade. On the contrary, he has repeatedly blamed Western powers for their aggressive behavior against Islam.

We can read his emphasis on mercy in the context of financial violence and European austerity that is destroying the life and future of the Greek people—and not only theirs. We can also read the emphasis on mercy in relation to the selfishness of European countries who refuse to accept migrants fleeing countries like Syria, Iraq, and Afghanistan, countries pushed into an abyss by infinite Western wars.

As I do not expect redemption in my afterlife, I think that despair is the only appropriate intellectual stance in this time. But I also think that despair and joy are not irreconcilable, as despair is the mood of the intellectual mind, while joy is the mood of the embodied mind. Friendship is the force that transforms despair into joy. This is the lesson that I learn from the man who came from the end of the world.

GLOBAL CIVIL WAR:
Is There Any Way Out?

2016

NECRO-ECONOMY

Are we heading towards a Third World War? Yes and no. War has been with us since the start of the twentieth century, it promises to be with us for a long time, and it threatens to destroy the last remnants of modern civilization. The exacerbation of xenophobia across the West and the rise of nationalism in countries like France are causes and effects of a looming war whose sources lie in the past two hundred years of colonial impoverishment and the humiliation of much of the world's population, not to mention neoliberal competition and the privatization of everything, including war itself.

Pacifism is becoming irrelevant as the conditions of war become irreversible. How can we oppose war when killers shoot at a peaceful crowd at a concert? War is becoming normalized. Even the stock exchange no longer reacts to massacres. Its main concern is the looming stagnation of the world economy. After every armed attack, whether by Islamic fundamentalists or white supremacists, whether random murderers or by well-trained killers, Americans run to buy more weapons.

A Republican assemblywoman from Nevada named Michele Fiore recently posted a Christmas family portrait on Facebook. At first glance, it's like any other holiday card, with three generations of a family in red shirts and jeans in front of a Christmas tree. Upon closer inspection, you see that Mrs. Fiore, her adult daughters, their husbands, and even one of her grandchildren are all holding firearms. The privatization of war is an obvious feature of neoliberal deregulation, and the same paradigm has generated Halliburton and the Sinaloa Cartel, Blackwater and Daesh. The business of violence is one of the main branches of the global economy, and financial abstraction does not discriminate criminal money from any other kind.

The process of externalization and privatization is now provoking a worldwide civil war that is feeding itself. According to Nicholas Kristof, "in the last four years, more people have died in the United States from guns (including suicides and accidents) than

Americans have died in the wars in Korea, Vietnam, Afghanistan and Iraq combined."[1]

GLOBAL FRAGMENTARY CIVIL WAR

Are we heading toward a global war? Not exactly: no declarations of war are being issued, but innumerable combat zones are proliferating. No unified fronts are in sight, but fragmented micro-conflicts and uncanny alliances with no general strategic vision abound. "World war" is not the term for this. I would call it fragmentary global civil war.

And the fragments are not converging, because war is everywhere.

Now, as US Defense Secretary Ashton Carter claims, "destructive power of greater and greater magnitude falls into the hands of smaller and smaller groups of human beings."[2]

When war is privatized, no geopolitical order in the world can be imagined, no arrangement among the conflicting religious tribes can be pursued. No beginning and no end—an endless war, as bin Laden promised.

Some American Republicans claim that the killings are related to mental illness. In a way, they are right. But they misunderstand the causes and the extent of what they label mental illness. Mental illness is not the rare malady of an isolated dropout, but the widespread consequence of panic, depression, precariousness, and humiliation: These are the sources of the contemporary global fragmentary war, and they are spreading everywhere, rooted in the legacy of colonialism and in the frenzy of daily competition.

Neoliberal deregulation has opened the way to a regime of worldwide necro-economy: the all-encompassing law of competition has canceled out moral prescriptions and legal regulations.

1. Nicholas Kristof, "On Guns, We're Not Even Trying," *New York Times*, December 5, 2015.
2. "Discussion with Secretary Carter at the John F. Kennedy Jr. Forum, Harvard Institute of Politics, Cambridge, Massachusetts", defense.gov, December 1, 2015.

Since its earliest phases, Thatcher's neoliberal philosophy prescribed war among individuals. Hobbes, Darwin, and Hayek have all been summoned to conceptualize the end of social civilization, the end of peace.

Forget about the religious or ideological labels of the agents of massive violence and look instead at their true nature. Take the Sinaloa Cartel and Daesh and compare them to Blackwater and Exxon Mobil. They have much more in common than you may think. Their common goal is to extract the maximum amount of money from their investments in the most exciting products of the contemporary economy: terror, horror, and death. Necro-capitalism is the emerging economic order of the world.

Narco business is a pillar of the Mexican economy, and in fact the head of the Sinaloa Cartel, Joaquín "El Chapo" Guzmán, was listed by *Fortune* magazine as one of the most prominent businessmen of 2012. Why not? After all, he is just a neoliberal entrepreneur who deals in deregulated kidnappings, drug trafficking, and murder. Like neoliberal corporations investing money in the ultimate business, the Iraqi-Syrian caliphate and the Mexican narco-army pay salaries to their soldiers, who are necro-proletarians. The narco business recruits unemployed young men from Monterrey, Sinaloa, and Veracruz. The caliphate recruits young men from the suburbs of London, Cairo, Tunis, and Paris, then trains them to kidnap and slaughter people at random. Daesh salaries have been estimated to be as much as $1000 a month. The group acquires this money from ransom, oil, and taxes that have been imposed on millions of Sunni people. They deliver a postmodern medievalism, but one that is not at all backwards. On the contrary, it is an anticipation of the future.

In a video released by Dubiq, the advertising agency of the Islamic State, the rhetoric is the same as any other type of advertising: buy this product and you'll be happy. Multiple camera angles, slick graphics, slow motion, and even artificial wind give the whole thing a more dramatic mood: Join the cause and you'll find friends, warmth, and well-being. Jihad is the best therapy for depression.

A message for feeble-minded people, for suffering people craving warmth, virile friendship, belonging. Not so different from the ads that we see every day on the streets of Western cities, only more sincere when it comes to the subject of suicide. Suicide is crucial in this video: 6,500 current or former US military soldiers commit suicide each year, according to Dubiq. While Americans die alone in anger and despair, God's soldiers die eager to meet some seventy virgins waiting in Paradise to fuck them.

A BLUEPRINT FOR EUROPE AND THE WORLD

Do you remember Yugoslavia? For some time, it was a rather healthy federation of twenty-five million people. Different ethnic and religious communities coexisted, factories were managed by workers, everybody had a privately owned house, and very few suffered from hunger. Then came the International Monetary Fund, the Polish pope pushing Croatians into religious war against the Orthodox Serbs, and Germany delivering weapons to the fascist Ustaše.

In 1990, the United States cut off all forms of credit to Yugoslavia unless separate elections were held in each state of the federation within six months. As a consequence, Yugoslavia—no longer able to conduct foreign trade—was condemned to commercial bankruptcy, which reinforced the divisive tendencies of its states. The US then funded the individual states to dissolve the federation, also supporting parties and movements that promoted this process. Meanwhile, Germany shipped arms to Slovenia, Croatia, Bosnia, and Herzegovina. In March of 1991, fascist organizations in Croatia called for the overthrow of the Socialist government and the expulsion of all Serbs. On March 5, 1991, they attacked the federal army base at Gospić, and civil war began.

The extreme right-wing Croatian party Democratic Union, which used the flag, emblems, and slogans of the pro-Nazi Ustaše party, seized power. Citizenship, property rights, employment, retirement benefits, and passports were granted to Croats and to no other ethnic group. Thus, 300,000 Serbs armed themselves and entered the fray with unspeakable brutality.

The destruction of Yugoslavia can be seen as a return of Hitler's ghost to the world stage. Ethnic-religious wars caused around

170,000 casualties, as ethnic cleansing was practiced in every area of the federation. After seven years of violence, a new state order emerged, based on a paradigm of ethnic-religious identification, a principle thought to have been extinct after the end of the Second World War and the defeat of Nazism.

Twenty years after the Nazi-neoliberal wars of Yugoslavia, in all those small nation-states (except, perhaps, Slovenia) unemployment is rampant, people are impoverished, schools are privatized, and public infrastructure is in disrepair. Today, the Yugoslavia of the '90s may well be a blueprint for the European future: German Ordoliberalism has impoverished social life, depleted public services all over the continent, and inflicted humiliation on Syriza in Greece, which has jeopardized the core of European solidarity.

The failure to deal with the new wave of migrants from the East has exposed the political fragility of the European Union and now fuels a new outburst of fear, racism, shame, and bad conscience.

The icy wind of financial abstraction is instilling in the European soul a sense of desolation that Michel Houellebecq has described in his books. *La soumission* (*Submission*) is a novel about the sadness that emerges from the vanishing of collective desire, for example. Submission to the Supreme Entity (be it God or the market) is the source of the present gloom and the source of the present war.

Globalization has brought about the obliteration of modern universalism: capital flows freely everywhere and the labor market is globally unified, but this has not led to the free circulation of women and men, nor to the affirmation of universal reason in the world. Rather, the opposite is happening: As the intellectual energies of society are captured by the network of financial abstraction, as cognitive labor is subjugated to the abstract law of valorization, and as human communication is transformed into abstract interaction among disembodied digital agents, the social body is detached from the general intellect. The subsumption of the general intellect into the corporate kingdom of abstraction is depriving the living community of intelligence, understanding, and emotion.

And the brainless body reacts—on one side, a huge wave of mental suffering, and on the other side, the much-advertised cure for depression: fanaticism, fascism, and war. And, at the end, suicide.

BLU'S ICONOCLASM:
After Dada

2016

On November 26, 2016, the fortieth anniversary of the release of "Anarchy in the UK" by the Sex Pistols, the UK activist Joe Corré will burn his £5 million collection of punk memorabilia. This gesture by the son of Malcom McLaren and Vivian Westwood—two icons of punk's first wave—is a response to Punk London, a year-long slate of concerts, films, talks, and exhibitions organized by the British tourism board. As Corré explained to *NME Magazine*:

> You talk to people about it these days and it's almost like *Antiques Roadshow*. "I wish I kept those bondage trousers, they'd be worth a fortune now." What's that got to do with anything? That's why I think it's appropriate [to burn the collection] – to say punk rock is extinct. Otherwise, it's all going to end up in some tourist shop, in a glass case, like the Hard Rock Café or something, and they'll be selling "God Save The Queen" mugs with a safety pin through her nose at Buckingham Palace. ... To see punk ideas appropriated by the establishment... punk rock was never that. ... The point is that we don't pray to that altar, we don't pray to altar of money.[1]

As inspiration for his own conflagration, Corré cites The KLF's decision to burn a million pounds sterling in 1992, as documented in the film *Watch the K Foundation Burn a Million Quid*. The bonfire of punk-historical assets in November by Corré won't only be a refusal of value, however; it will also be a destruction of artifacts and, for Corré, a certain erasure of self.

The street artist Blu recently performed a similar gesture of consistent iconoclasm, nine hundred miles away in Bologna—a city very different from London. London is a huge metropolis, while Bologna is relatively small. London is frantically busy; Bologna is lazier. London is gargantuan and neuropathic; Bologna is more polluted, but less monstrous. There was a moment, however, when Bologna and London played similar roles in the zeitgeist. This was 1977, when

1. Leonie Cooper, "Joe Corré, Son of Malcolm McLaren and Vivienne Westwood, On Why He's Burning His £5 Million Punk Collection," *NME*, March 18, 2016.

two similar yet contrasting insurrections took place in the two cities, paving the way for a new imagination of the future. The London punk insurrection was dressed predominantly in black, while the Bologna autonomous insurrection was full of color; but the insurgents were part of the same precarious life. The London punks shouted "no future!" while the Bologna autonomists shouted "the future is now!"

Bologna is an interesting city. At the end of the Middle Ages, *clerici vagantes* (wandering artists) from the south and the north gathered there and founded what is said to have been the first university of the modern world, the University of Bologna. For generations, new waves of scientists and artists, poets and social rebels have traversed the city's streets: they have been a nomadic minority where most of the population has been busy with commerce and industry.

Over the centuries, the local authorities have dealt in different ways with this nomadic intellectual minority. Often, they have tried to repress, marginalize, and sometimes expel these innovators, those enemies of the established order. At other times, the local bourgeoisie have tried to take advantage of the creativity of the nomadic outlaws.

But the richness of the city rests upon the nomadic brain that gathers and disperses, leaving traces of its passage: artworks, inventions, technical and political innovations. So it happens that in certain periods the city is ebullient and inventive. In other periods, however, the nomadic brilliance vanishes, and butchers, bureaucrats, and bankers occupy the scene, exploiting the products of the nomadic innovators and transforming work into money, creation into value, and art into the Museum.

In the late twentieth century, a wave of cultural unrest and political rebellion swept Bologna: poets and activists and technological innovators revived the early twentieth-century artistic vanguard and mixed it with a freshly imagined social autonomy. Dadaism had a presence in the streets of Bologna in the 1970s, when thousands of students, young workers, and women decided to refuse their destiny of exploitation and sadness and tried to transform daily life into an artwork.

"Mao-Dadaism" detonated in the '70s as a double ironic prank. It was a way to declare that Maoism and the entire Communist legacy of the twentieth century was a funny remnant of an epoch that was fading away. But it was also a way to marry the tragic thread of communist revolution to the crazy thread of artistic ambiguousness. The ironic Mao-Dada rebellion exploded in 1977: For three days, police tanks tried to remove thousands of young rebels from the university quarter in Bologna. In the end they succeeded, after killing a student, arresting more than three hundred people, and shutting down a pirate radio station that was promulgating the schizo-utopian transformation of daily life.

This was the last proletarian insurgency of the communist century in Europe, but it was simultaneously the first insurrection of the precarious cognitariat, based on the intuition that the modern imagination of the future was dissolving.

The separation of art and daily life was the enemy of the Mao-Dada rebels. We—for I was one—did not care much about politics, governments, and power. Our mission was to break the separation between art and daily life, in the spirit of Tristan Tzara, the Romanian-French poet who was accused of being a purveyor of odalisques, narcotics, and scandalous literature. In the spring of 1916, while war raged all over Europe, Tzara launched the Dada project at the Cabaret Voltaire, declaring: “Abolish art, abolish daily life, abolish the separation between art and daily life.”

Lenin was sitting somewhere in the same cabaret, sipping tea or vodka—I don’t remember which. What would the history of the century have been if the poet and the communist became friends with the Dadaists and learned their ironic style? Would the century have been lighter? Maybe. Dadaist irony might have been a useful antidote to Bolshevik severity.

Rhetorically, at least, the two shared an attachment to immanence, or at the very least a suspicion of traditional forms of representation. Writing one year later in *State and Revolution*, Lenin used language not so different from Tzara’s to insist on “the *smashing*, the *destruction*” of bourgeois parliamentarianism, which also separated everyday life from what claimed to represent it.[2]

2. Vladimir Ilyich Lenin, *The State and Revolution* (Mineola, NY: Dover, [1917] 2021), 40.

"We cannot imagine democracy, even proletarian democracy, without representative institutions, but we can and must imagine democracy without parliamentarism," wrote Lenin.[3] Such a vision of democracy shares with the Cabaret Voltaire the refusal of separation, and the destruction of the distinction between audience and performer, whether that be understood as spectator/artist or citizen/representative.

The distinction between the Dadaist and Leninist vanguards lies not in the goal, but in the method. It is the difference between an amateur cabaret and a vanguard party of professional revolutionaries. In the first case, it is the space of art as a distinct professional realm that is invaded by the unskilled forces of everyday life. In the second, it is the space of everyday life that is occupied by the imperatives of the professional revolutionary. Lenin's phrase "Everything within the party, nothing without" is a reversal of the Dadaist gesture. Rather than letting everyday life into the theater to crush the division between the audience and the performer, the vanguard party expands outwards to include the audience among its ranks. In other words, both theories seek the destruction of the professional/amateur distinction, but the Dadaist strategy pursues this goal by championing amateurism and enacting a certain *classlessness*, while Leninism seeks the triumph of the revolutionary professional.

Naturally, the precarious classes that composed the Mao-Dadaists of '77 tried to change the course of history by returning to the immanent co-participation of art and everyday life promised by Dada. But this required acting *autonomously* from the leadership of the Communist Party, whose existence as an institutionalized, professional vanguard placed it in conflict with a movement of the precarious who were, like Dada, aligned against professionalism, which they understood as the force separating art and life. But it was too late. In those years, the planet was already running out of a future.

At the beginning of the twenty-first century, when the storm of '77 was already a fading memory, Blu came to Bologna as a nomadic artist. He went to the Museum of Natural History and saw prehistoric fish with long teeth and reptilian scales. He went to anarchist meetings in

3. Lenin, 50.

squatted houses like XM24. At night he painted on the walls of suburban buildings, abandoned factories, ghosts of extinguished industrial capitalism. The paintings were full of primordial and aggressive animals, late-modern warriors, and squatters living in moonless cavities. On the walls of derelict dwellings, he painted skyscrapers and armies of menacing tanks, shy elephants and aggressive turtles.

In the last ten years, Blu has painted graffiti in Berlin, Los Angeles, and Rome, but in Bologna his paintings are visible in so many places that his style marks the cityscape.

However, life in the city of Bologna is not easy for people like Blu. Local authorities and the racist local newspaper *il Resto del Carlino* have repeatedly denounced street artists as vandals, subverters, and allies of the anarcho-autonomous squatters. Time and again, squads of cleaners have walked around the city to erase the graffiti on the walls.

But then, something more dramatic happened, after which all of Blu's pieces in Bologna disappeared, covered up with gray paint. It was not an act of repression, nor was it because of the bigotry of good citizens who love order and clean walls. Instead, the works disappeared through an act of self-erasure. On the night of March 11, 2016, on the thirty-ninth anniversary of the massive riots that followed the killing of the student Francesco Lorusso by the police, Blu, helped by a group of activists, covered over his own works with gray paint. But why?

A week later, on March 18, an exhibition called "Street Art: Banksy & Co." was scheduled to open. The exhibition was organized by the Fondazione Carisbo, a local foundation owned by a bank whose president is Fabio Roversi Monaco, the former rector of the University of Bologna as well as the former president of BolognaFiere, a public-private partnership that organizes exhibitions. In Bologna, the name Roversi Monaco evokes power, money, and banks. The exhibition was expected to display works of art removed from walls with the stated intention of "salvaging them from demolition and preserving them from the injuries of time," which means turning them into museum pieces and eventually transforming them into value.[4]

4. See Wu Ming, "Street Artist #Blu Is Erasing All The Murals He Painted in #Bologna," wumingfoundation.com, March 12, 2016.

The situation perfectly epitomized the old story of separating art from daily life and of the museification of art separated from life. After his action of self-erasure, Blu published a statement on Wu Ming's blog, writing: "After having denounced and criminalized graffiti as vandalism, after having oppressed the youth culture that created them, after having evacuated the places which functioned as laboratories for those artists, now Bologna's powers-that-be pose as the saviors of street art."

Street artists have been repeatedly denounced and arrested in Bologna. Two have been jailed, and many more have been fined. Recently, the mayor of Bologna welcomed a delegation of volunteers who had taken part in a "no tag" clean-up project against "graphic vandalism," organized by the Bologna government to the town hall. The municipality even pays building owners who remove graffiti from the walls of their properties.

Then the Museum comes to the rescue of what is left of street art, with the Bank supporting the expropriation.

Is Roversi Monaco's act of expropriation legal? Yes, he claims: "We've asked permission from the legitimate owners of the derelict buildings these murals were on." But Roversi Monaco has also conceded: "The artist remains the author, but the owner is whoever owns the building."

Thus, Blu decided to opt out of the show.

Blu's action was performed almost exactly one hundred years after the birth of Dada, and so I read it as the final self-erasure of the historical vanguard. The long-standing attempt to translate art into life, and to transform life into art, is over. It was an ambiguous, dangerous project. The will for art-life cross-contamination produced contradictory effects throughout the past century. It fueled countless collective and individual insurrections that traversed the existence of millions of rebellious bodies, millions of workers refusing to work. But it also nourished advertising, the ceaseless flow of semiotic pollution in the infosphere. Aesthetic innovation and the market have played a game of reciprocal plundering, with the Museum, especially the Bank-Museum, swallowing life and transforming it into abstraction.

Blu's act is a sort of self-deleting of a dynamic century. It is not the Museum but the gray wall that will reactivate the depressed imagination of our times. A gray wall, like a bonfire, is a sacrifice that leaves behind a suggestion: Do not continue the game, start a new one. Do not build on the ruins of past "modern" values. Abandon illusions, get prepared for the perfect storm. And in the storm—if I may conclude with Bob Marley—emancipate yourself from mental slavery, none but yourself can free your mind.

This text has been written in collaboration with MARCO MAGAGNOLI, president of the Cultural Association Menomale, which is dedicated to the theory and technology of immersive media. He is the creator of The Look of Life, a video website for people who live in contexts of isolation.

ENGINEERING SELF

2016

COGNITIVE AUTOMATION AND ENGINEERING OF THE SELF

Observing his subatomic self... no chronology was stable.

—Jonathan Franzen, *Purity*[1]

A knower, by whatever name one may want to call it—self, experiencer, protagonist—needs to be generated in the brain if the mind is to become conscious. When the brain manages to introduce a knower in the mind, subjectivity follows.

—Antonio Damasio, *Self Comes to Mind*[2]

Contemporary technological development tends to move towards behavioral and cognitive automation. I want to speak about the concept of "self-design" in this context; however these two words, "self" and "design," need elaboration. Their meanings are far from obvious and, indeed, are changing dramatically. "Self-design" can be thought of as the authorship of one's own subjectivity. Yet I would argue that in today's digital context, what is most politically urgent is what I would term the "hetero-design" of the self. The self, insofar as it is conceived as a simulation, is turned into an effect of automated design or engineering, and thus cognitive behavior is more and more the outcome of technical simulation.

The word "design" essentially refers to the relation between objects and utility. Design, in this sense, encompasses both conceptual art and engineering: as art, design conceives a world for an object, and as engineering, design builds an object for the world. As a hegemonic process of production, semiocapitalism is predicated on the redesign of processes of relation, such as cooperation. Today,

1. Jonathan Franzen, *Purity* (New York: Farrar, Straus and Giroux, 2015).
2. Antonio Damasio, *Self Comes to Mind: Constructing the Conscious Brain* (New York: Random House, 2011).

technical interfaces connect segments of society, both human and electronic, lubricating the social body and automating activity. How does this process affect the reflective function of the human, the "self?" How does this process affect consciousness, the self-reflexive function of cognition?

In order to address the significance of the engineering of the self, we must first differentiate it from the ego. Ego is the agent, the actor, the sufferer. The self, on the other hand, is the interior scene where volition—the will to act—comes to be. The processes that made the self "modern" were essentially based on the manipulation of the conjunctive space between bodies and embodied minds. In speaking about "technologies of the self," Michel Foucault reveals how practices like prayer, reading, and political participation have shaped the individual mind to allow for social evolution. In contrast to the institutional forms he unveiled as constitutive of the modern subject, in his later years Foucault became increasingly aware of a new dimension of subjectivation. Whereas mechanisms of control and the rules of political order might have once primarily resided in institutional forms, they have come to be embedded within the social body itself.

Foucault's intuition paved the way for the investigation of a social mutation that is currently taking place as a result of the deepening penetration of digital technology into the molecular fabric of subjectivity. Whereas design used to imply the conjunction and blending of language, emotion, and touch in the digital age, design does none of this. Instead, design generates chains of signification, the comprehension of which shapes cognitive protocols of re-cognition and habit. The current evolution of digital technology is transforming the human environment in such a way that the very relation between the ego—as actor—and the self—as mirror—is being reformatted.

The reflective function of the self investigates the ego and the contexts, meaning, ethics, and implications of its actions. Yet what if that space of action is technically fabricated, simulated?[3] Digitization

3. And what if that scene becomes projected onto the screen of the mind, as in *The Matrix*?

substitutes the human ability of conjunction for connection, insertion, and the contribution to chains of automatic signification. What is at stake in the modal shift from conjunction to connection is concatenation; ultimately, the power of human communication, interaction, and signification. We can study this mutation through the lens of two technological developments currently taking place: data management and immersive environments. While on the one hand the implementation of big-data storage, mining, and forms of algorithmic governance that have emerged from such processes externalize the act of reflection, disarm the self, and allow the body to be captured by statistical projection, on the other, virtual reality reformats the very relation between the self and the unconscious.

DATIFICATION AND STATISTICAL PRE-SCRIPTION

The future is inscribed in the present state of the world, and particularly in the present state of our minds. Foucault observed in *Discipline and Punish* that by individualizing subjects and placing them in a state of constant visibility, power can control behavior. Jeremy Bentham's Panopticon penitentiary was the architectural manifestation of this machine of constant visibility. With information flows intensifying and social life becoming more complex (and less predictable), control has become more difficult. Yet statistical patterns can be extracted from huge data records of social behavior and successively projected back onto the social organism. Warren Neidich calls this cycle the "Statisticon":

> The term Statisticon describes a process of subjectivation and subjection that commences with the panopticon, continues through the Synopticon and has recently emerged as the Statisticon in which architecture and designed space are entangled in synchronous and diachronous datascapes.[4]

4. Warren Neidich, "Computational Architecture and the Statisticon," in *Psychopathologies of Cognitive Capitalism: Part Two* (Berlin: Archive Books, 2014), 339.

Following Neidich, contemporary power has become increasingly spatial. Public space has effectively become the urban condition that the architecture and urban design practice MVRDV identified in 1999 as *Metacity/Datatown*, whose origins Matteo Pasquinelli traces to the literary imagination of William Gibson: "The buildings of the cyberspace were originally blocks of data, and if they resembled three-dimensional objects, it was only to domesticate and colonize an abstract space—that is, the abstract space of any augmented mind."[5]

The Statisticon thus reformats subjectivity insofar as it transforms the perception of space. In the essay "Régimen de visibilidad y vigilancia en la era de la Identidad Digital" (Regime of visibility and vigilance in the era of digital identity), María Alejandra López Gabrielidis investigates the relation between data and identity in terms of a special sort of reification that she properly names "datification."[6] According to López Gabrielidis, reification spawns from the perception of one's body as an external thing. Thanks to the possibility of recording, storing, and replaying huge amounts of data picked from the daily behavior of human populations, this process of self-reification is shifting from the stage of the passive, reflective mirror, one that resides within the subject, to one that is interactive, external, and capable of driving the actor to comply. López Gabrielidis observes that data reification implies the externalization of traits of individuation, engendering "a second support of presence, that might be named 'datified self.'"[7]

Following the introduction of filter bubbles, as defined by Eli Pariser, statistical recording turns into prescription. Contemporary powers aim to reduce future behavioral possibilities to predicable models, the potential for which lies in its ability to routinely read big flows of data. As Pasquinelli describes:

5. Matteo Pasquinelli, "Anomaly Detection: The Mathematization of the Abnormal in the Metadata Society," talk at *Transmediale Festival*, Berlin, January 29, 2015, published in *Anthropocene Curriculum*, April 23, 2016.
6. María Alejandra López Gabrielidis, "Régimen de visibilidad y vigilancia en la era de la Identidad Digital," *Teknokultura. Revista de Cultura Digital y Movimientos Sociales* 12, no. 3 (2015), 473–499.
7. López Gabrielidis, "Régimen de visibilidad y vigilancia en la era de la Identidad Digital."

> The two epistemic poles of pattern and anomaly are the two sides of the same coin of algorithmic governance. An unexpected anomaly can be detected only against the background of pattern regularity. Conversely, a pattern emerges only through the median equalization of diverse tendencies.[8]

As massive flows of data are recorded, the machine can adapt to the living environment and affect the reciprocal adaptation of conscious organisms to the machine. Techniques of customization enable Google and other search engines not just to anticipate our requests, but also to shape and control our desires. Preemption is complementary to statistical capture; preempting the future means emptying future behavior of singularity. Statistical preemption is the functional mode of governance—the contemporary form of political and economic power—that may be defined as a form of engendered determinism.

IMMERSION

The Statisticon externalizes the self and turns inscription—data extracted from social life and recorded in the interactive mirror—into prescription. But the current engineering of the self also involves an internal process of cognitive reformation, exemplified by immersive technologies such as virtual reality.

In the 1980s, Jaron Lanier spoke for the first time of communication without symbols, implying the possibility of exchanging meaning with images and various noetic contents without transferring conventional signifiers. In 1991, Pierre Levy, in the visionary book *L'ideographie Dynamique*, imagined the possibility of transferring perceptions directly from one brain to another by stimulating specific neuronal pathways that correspond to those perceptions. Also in the 1990s, the first data gloves enabled users to corporeally receive audio-visual stimulation and have simulated experiences, like walking on a square planet or throwing and catching a non-existent ball.

At first, the dawn of the World Wide Web wiped away interests in such forms of technology, but now, immersion is back. Virtual environments currently play an important role in military combat training, flight simulation, and medical surgery.The now-infamous photo of Mark Zuckerberg walking alone in a crowd of users wearing blinking plastic masks speaks volumes about the coming mass production of the environment by a techno-elite. As the physical environment of cities decay and their social environments becomes increasingly miserable, can we not already catch glimpses of a populational migration to simulations? From a psychological point of view, this decentering of the self may lead to a confusion of heterogenous perception and automated cognitive action. Google Maps has already fundamentally altered our sense of spatial orientation. Downloading entails the end of the linear transmission of information—the sequential transmission of symbolic contents—and its replacement by the immediate transfer of experience and knowledge.

In the alphabetical age, the perception of time could be represented by a transition in our visual field from left to right: from before to after, with the present in the center, proceeding towards the future. As immersive environments replace alphabetical text, time is going to become the dimension in which countless non-hierarchical instants flow. No page has to be turned anymore; the infinite scroll of an immersive screen has neither beginning nor end, but suddenly enlightens a point that does not exist. No more spectators or readers, but rather travelers who experience the world that someone else imagined. Might we not be able to imagine a different future, in which curiosity replaces hope (as hope has lost any ground in the precarious age), and deviate from automation? We tend to dismiss the potential of exploration in these spaces. But lines of escape from our oppressive and depressing reality can be found in this dimension.

THE COMING '17

2016

THE INTERMINABLE COLLAPSE

The hundredth anniversary of the Soviet Revolution will likely coincide with a global collapse. The oft-announced recovery is not coming, and a right-wing wave with racist undertones is mounting. The collapse of capitalism will be interminable and enormously destructive as long as a new subjectivity does not emerge and a different social model does not develop. The subjectivity expressed in the nineteenth century by the workers' movement appears today so disintegrated that we cannot imagine any possible recomposition in the near future.

The anti-finance uprisings of 2011 have not succeeded in reversing the route of financial plunder, and the European leftist parties have accepted austerity politics, even if this betrayal is likely to provoke their final defeat.

The dynamics that led to the ascent of the Nazis and then to the Second World War are back. Contemporary nationalist parties are echoing what Hitler said to the impoverished workers of Germany: You are not defeated and exploited workers, but national warriors, and you will win. They did not win, but they did destroy Europe. They will not win this time either, but they are poised to destroy the world.

The ongoing impoverishment of society is not a natural inevitability, but a consequence of the politics of financial accumulation. The neoliberal model implements itself by force of automatism, while consensus melts away. The July 2016 issue of *The Economist* had the theme "Anarchy in the UK" and admitted the bankruptcy of neoliberal globalism. The symptoms are visible: stagnation, overproduction, and then deflation and looming recession.

The sources of stagnation and unemployment—market saturation and the reduction of necessary labor time—are not inherently negative trends in themselves. On the contrary, from the perspective of social usefulness, they prove that the era of scarcity is over and that the emancipation of human time from repetitive work is imminent. The material basis now exists for people to devote their time to the care of others, self-care, education, and other non-market activities.

Capitalism, however, is semiotically unable to implement the potentialities inherent to knowledge and technology: Its dynamic tends in fact to contain those potentialities within old frameworks of growth and accumulation. Consequently, it transforms the potentialities of knowledge and technology into factors of scarcity and destruction.

This distortion has impoverished European society and is unleashing an antiglobal reaction that is feeding resentment, fascism, and war. What will happen next?

1917 WILL NOT HAPPEN AGAIN

In the age of bio-info political power, the Winter Palace is empty. But we must revisit 1917, because the Soviet Revolution established the paradigm that presided over the political landscape of the last century: the working class organized via political parties into a social vanguard, seeking to seize power and use it against the capitalist class. The vision that Lenin expressed in his writings (particularly in *What Is to Be Done?*) provided a military framework for class struggle. This tactical move allowed the Bolshevik party to seize power, but this was also Lenin's strategic mistake, and maybe his crime. The Leninist party gave birth to a state and an army, but Lenin's determination turned class struggle into war, thereby suffocating the processes of revolutionary autonomy in Germany, Italy, and in the United States, where the Industrial Workers of the World were expanding their social organization.

In order to win the war unleashed by the Leninist revolution, Western capitalism fomented fascism against the working class. We know the story of what followed: Soviet Communism and Anglo-American capitalism were forced into an alliance. In the second half of the century, democracy emerged as the victorious mythology, but its triumph did not last. Beginning in Chile on September 11, 1973, the neoliberal reformation started canceling democracy there and went on to cancel democracy everywhere else (including in Greece in July 2015). The dictatorship of the abstract over concrete life emerged under the label of neoliberal governance, which thrived more or less peacefully until the end of the '90s. Since the dot-com crash of spring 2000 and the new September 11 of the first year of the new century, the global landscape has fragmented into countless conflicting identities that are now exploding into a global civil war.

COLONIALISM AND INTERNATIONALISM

Zbigniew Brzezinski, former adviser to US President Jimmy Carter, has written important books about the global political landscape. In 1993, he published *Out of Control: Global Turmoil on the Eve of the 21st Century*, a book in which he subverted the prevailing optimism of that period and predicted the uncontrollable proliferation of identitarian conflict.

In a recent issue of *The American Interest*, Brzezinski published an essay entitled "Toward a Global Realignment." Notwithstanding the flavorless title, the article contains a dramatic consideration that may be summarized as follows: After centuries of colonial domination and violence, the former colonies are asking for moral and economic restitution that the West is unwilling and unable to pay. The concrete historical debt we owe to those we have exploited cannot be paid, because we are forced to pay our abstract financial debts.

Brzezinski's style in the essay is elegant, but his words are appalling and unequivocal:

> Special attention should be focused on the non-Western world's newly politically aroused masses. Long-repressed political memories are fueling in large part the sudden and very explosive awakening energized by Islamic extremists in the Middle East, but what is happening in the Middle East today may be just the beginning of a wider phenomenon to come out of Africa, Asia, and even among the pre-colonial peoples of the Western Hemisphere in the years ahead.
>
> Periodic massacres of their not-so-distant ancestors by colonists and associated wealth-seekers largely from western Europe (countries that today are, still tentatively

> at least, most open to multiethnic cohabitation) resulted within the past two or so centuries in the slaughter of colonized peoples on a scale comparable to Nazi World War II crimes: literally involving hundreds of thousands and even millions of victims.[1]

I agree with Brzezinski's diagnosis, but he forgets to say that in the twentieth century, internationalism emerged to avert the kind of global conflict he describes. Only the workers' internationalist sentiment could avoid planetary bloodbath. But communism has been defeated, and the internationalist way has dissolved. We now face a war of all against all for the sake of nothing.

DEPRESSED SUBJECTIVITY

After the dissolution of communism, the mythology of boundless competition and profit gained the upper hand. But after thirty years, this mythology has gone totally bankrupt. Western subjectivity is angrily depressed. As Jonathan Franzen explains from the US perspective:

> People came to this country for either money or freedom. If you don't have money, you cling to your freedoms all the more angrily. Even if smoking kills you, even if you can't afford to feed your kids, even if your kids are getting shot down by maniacs with assault rifles. You may be poor, but the one thing nobody can take away from you is the freedom to fuck up your life whatever way you want to. That's what Bill Clinton figured out—that we can't win elections by running against personal liberties. Especially not against guns, actually.[2]

1. Zbigniew Brzezinski, "Toward a Global Realignment," *The American Interest* 11, no. 6 (July–August 2016).
2. Jonathan Franzen, *Freedom* (New York: Farrar, Straus and Giroux, 2011), 361.

The promise of economic success has been achieved by only a small part of society. For the losers, it has resulted in precariousness, neuro-exploitation, a diminishing salary, and more work. But the losers are reclaiming their personal freedoms, and in the US this means, first and foremost, the freedom to keep and bear arms.

With the dissolving of the internationalist vision, everybody now belongs to a clan—ethnic or virtual—and everybody is preparing to protect themselves against the coming invasion. After the abandonment of the universalist horizon of enlightened modernity, conflicting subjectivities are now kept together by a faith in belonging.

PROGRAM

Since mental activity is captured by the economy, and the bulk of contemporary work is semiotic, reflection is absorbed and assimilated and reduced to work. In the past, industrial workers were not directly engaged in their tasks mentally. Contemporary semioworkers, however, are obliged to engage their mental faculties in the automated process of production.

Only a break in the submission of cognitarian consciousness to the paradigm of competition can now open a process leading to the autonomous self-organization of cognitive labor. The emancipation of knowledge-force represents the only chance to defeat the neuro-totalitarian system in the making.

The task for the future is to reinvent the process of subjectivation. This reinvention must start from the spreading conditions of mental suffering and from the discovery of a new level of political action. The concept of a program has long been at the core of political action. In the last century, the word "program" referred to an organic ensemble of projects that politics enforced on the social body. Now we should think of "program" in terms of social software: an algorithm based on social needs and aimed at social welfare, which should oppose the financial algorithm prevailing today. Only an algorithm for emancipation can replace the present algorithm for financial exploitation.

Programming (in the sense of software for the production process) is the activity particular to cognitive workers. The autonomy of programming practices is the political project that we have to pursue. But we know that the autonomy of practices presupposes the autonomy of the subject.

In the global Silicon Valley, there are millions of cognitive workers worldwide: This is the subjectivity that can subvert financial dictatorship. We must view the global Silicon Valley in the same way that Lenin viewed the Putilov factory in 1917, and in the same way that autonomia rebels viewed the Mirafiori Fiat plant in '70s: as the core of the process of production, the place where the maximal level of exploitation is exerted and where the highest transformative potential can be unleashed.

While politics is impotent and nation-states cannot govern the flows of semiofinance, the global Silicon Valley has replaced the governments of the past. However, it is not a place without conflict: in this deterritorialized factory, millions of cognitive workers can develop a new form of consciousness and a new social dynamic based on the reduction of labor time, the uncoupling of income from work, and the full implementation of technology and automation. The challenge is to cultivate this consciousness among cognitive workers: From their mental suffering, an ethical awakening can arise. And in the ethical awakening of millions of engineers, artists, and scientists lies the only possibility of averting a frightening regression, whose contours we glimpse already.

THE SECOND COMING

2017

THE SECOND COMING OF WHAT?

The Congress of Versailles, 1919, can be viewed as the moment when the political landscape of modernity was fully shaped as a world-scape. In the same year, William Butler Yeats—referencing the apocalyptic postwar context—wrote “The Second Coming,” a poem about the collapse of social order and the decomposition of civilization. “Things fall apart; the centre cannot hold; / Mere anarchy is loosed upon the world.”[1]

In the years following the immense devastation of the First World War, Yeats speaks of the painful “blood-dimmed” chaos that is unleashed upon the world and sees a sign of the second coming of Jesus Christ. I’m reading Yeats from the point of view of today, 2017, and I want to interpret his words in a nontheological way, one hundred years after the beginning of the Russian Revolution, which aimed to eliminate war and exploitation from the history of the world but resulted in the creation of a miserable totalitarian regime of oppression.

The second coming of communism will happen on grounds that have nothing to do with Leninist force and Bolshevik coercion, nothing to do with political dictatorship. The second coming of communism will happen as an effect of the trauma that capitalism (and the capitalist use of technology) has inflicted on the human mind. Economic competition and obsessive accumulation have provoked violence, frustration, and war. Communism means ridding ourselves of the superstition of property and the superstition of salaried work. The redistribution of wealth and the emancipation of social time from the blackmail of salaried work: There is no other key to the future.

What happened in 2016 (Brexit, Trump, growing nationalist fervor in Europe, the spread of civil war across the globe) is jeopardizing the mental world-map inherited from the modern age. This is confirmed by an article entitled “Toward a Global Realignment”

1. W. B. Yeats, “The Second Coming,” in *The Collected Poems of W. B. Yeats* (1989). All quotes from Yeats in this text are from this poem.

by Zbigniew Brzezinski, published in *The American Interest* in June 2016. Until his death in May of this year, Brzezinski was a leading foreign policy intellectual, who for decades was an authoritative representative of the American establishment. According to Brzezinski, Daesh is only the beginning of a terrorist planetary war that will mark the current century. Westerners, Brzezinski says, have to realize that after five hundred years of predation, massacre, and humiliation, the colonized peoples of the world have started taking their revenge, launching religious and national wars everywhere. The oppressed of the world can now take revenge because of the accessibility of deadly and massively destructive weapons. After centuries of plunder and humiliation, the victims are reacting. On the other side, white Western workers, impoverished by the financial aggression of the last thirty years, are seeking social revenge and unleashing a global racial war. From an internationalist point of view, this is the worst-case scenario: a perfect recipe for the defeat of humanity.

Donald Trump's victory is the price that the white working class is willing to pay in order to take revenge against the neoliberal left. Humiliated people sometimes decide to identify with the humiliator in chief. Humiliated white US workers have chosen Trump because he is the humiliator of the humiliating neoliberal elite. They think, "he is our man because he is the one who knows best how to humiliate those who have cheated us."

UNAVOIDABLE AND UNPREDICTABLE

In the crystal ball of our century, it's easy to see an increase in war and exploitation. But we should not forget that the unavoidable usually does not happen, because, in history, it is the unpredictable that prevails.

Our first task as intellectuals is to describe the unavoidable. We have to look straight into the eyes of the beast. But, simultaneously, we have to remember that the game-changing event that opens a new view and new possibilities is unpredictable. The more complex a system is, the less we can predict the wide-ranging effects of a marginal cultural trend or an unknown technical discovery.

Thus, notwithstanding our feelings of despair, we should not stop exercising the art of thinking and the art of philosophical imagination. I know that in the age of communication and speed, thought is dismissed as an old habit. Thought seems ineffective and ornamental. But this is part of the unavoidable.

We should not stop thinking, because the unpredictable may soon need to be thought, and this is our job, our task: thinking in times of apocalyptic trauma. This is why we should not stop repeating the word *internationalism*. You know what internationalism is. When Lenin wrote that "capitalism brings war like clouds bring the storm," he knew that the First World War was unavoidable, and he knew that this unavoidability could only be subverted by the unpredictable: a workers' revolution. In 1914, while French and German socialists voted for war credits, succumbing to the rhetoric of patriotism and accepting national war, Lenin said no to the war. I've never been a Leninist, but I cannot deny that at the Zimmerwald Conference in 1915, Lenin was right.

Similarly today, despite the unavoidability of war, we must say no to the war. We must organize desertion and boycotts; we must prepare the overthrow of the system that has generated the war. Internationalism is not a moral value nor an ideology, but the materialist understanding of a simple fact: The workers of the world share a common interest, which is having more of what they produce and working less.

When workers are united in a social conflict, they can win. When they are captured by nationalist sentiment, when national fronts proliferate, war spreads and workers lose everything—no matter if they're German, French, American, or Russian. The rising nationalism of our time is an effect of the defeat that the working class has suffered; the betrayal by the neoliberal left has deprived the working class of all political defense. The neoliberal left bears the responsibility for the defeat of workers, for the impoverishment of society, and for the humiliation that is now turning people against progressive values. Many workers hate the Left (and rightly so), because it is identified with financial aggression and neoliberal cosmopolitan conformism.

Tony Blair is now trying to come back. He wrote a message to the British people, saying that Brexit was a mistake and that the mistake has to be mended. He will come back to help Britain behave. If I had to choose between Nigel Farage and Tony Blair, I would not choose Farage, but I wouldn't choose Blair either. It is the Blairist Left that has destroyed all trust in democracy.

THE CEREMONY OF INNOCENCE

Things fall apart; the centre cannot hold;
Mere anarchy is loosed upon the world,
The blood-dimmed tide is loosed, and everywhere
The ceremony of innocence is drowned;
The best lack all conviction, while the worst
Are full of passionate intensity.

—W. B. Yeats, "The Second Coming"

The line "The ceremony of innocence is drowned" makes me think of what is happening every day in the Mediterranean Sea, where innocent people are drowned by wars fueled by the West. This is free association, of course. Yeats could not have imagined the tragedy that war and migration are today provoking in the Mediterranean in our postmodern times.

European consciousness denies what is happening. Everywhere along the Mediterranean coast, concentration camps are built with EU money. In Turkey, in Libya, in Egypt, in those countries led by fascist murderers like Al-Sisi and Erdoğan, migrants are detained, tortured, enslaved, killed in those concentration camps that Europeans do not want to host on their soil.

In the 1940s, the majority of Europeans did not know and could not have known about Auschwitz. Now we know. Now, everybody in Europe knows that concentration camps are back. Europeans prefer to externalize the horror, to pay executioners who are far from the eyes of European children.

The Yeats poem unchains many meaningful if arbitrary associations: this is what poetry does. Meaningful arbitrariness is the gift that poetry offers to our minds. Serendipity in the process of meaning-making. Poetical ambiguousness is the vibrational condition that leads to conceptual discovery, to the imagination of other possible lands that we cannot see. What is happening in the Euro-Mediterranean will not be overcome in political terms. Political decision is impotent. What we need is a reactivation of human empathy, which is beyond politics. It's pre-political, or post-political, or meta-political; I don't know. If the majority of Europeans are unable to feel empathy for the thousands who have drowned in the Mediterranean in recent years, they are dangerously sick. And they are sick because of the long-lasting impoverishment that financial capitalism has produced in their lives. In such conditions of apathy and depression and fear, the political reason of governments cannot decide. And the wave of migration and despair will not stop crashing on the shores of our cursed continent-fortress.

THE LIMIT

"The best lack all conviction, while the worst / Are full of passionate intensity." The best? Who are the best that Yeats invokes? I think of people like Vittorio Arrigoni and Rachel Corrie, killed while defending Palestinians from Israeli aggression. They were part of the community of cultural nomads who want to "stay human," who sometimes come together in sudden conglomerations called "movements." They are not believers and do not pretend to belong to any truth. They are skeptical and ironic; they don't care about dogmas, convictions, or prejudices, so they look at reality with an ironic and tolerant gaze.

Wittgenstein says that the limits of our world are the limits of our language. Poetry is the enunciation that overcomes those limits. Poetry happens when language questions the limits of language. Poetry happens when these limits are surpassed by an excess of meaning, a meaning that limited language is unable to express. The potential richness of social knowledge and of technology is limited and perverted by the semiotic container of financial capitalism. Finance is a semiotic transformer of human activity, transforming richness into misery, inequality, and abstract accumulation. This is the limit that we are unable to surpass. It's firstly a semiotic limit.

We don't see the possibility that is inscribed in the present composition of labor, knowledge, and technology, because we are limited by the limits of our language, of our superstition: the superstition of salaried work. Our vision of the possible is limited by the preconception that if one wants to survive, one must work eight hours a day. This is the limit that we have to overcome, and poetry is the place where the research for this overcoming happens.

In a 2014 interview in *Computer World*, Larry Page said that Google already had intelligent devices that could replace 50 percent of existing jobs. 50 percent of existing jobs could disappear tomorrow if Silicon Valley implemented its current innovations. This implies that working eight hours a day makes no sense.

We are accustomed to listening to the discourse of the powerful, which is based on the idea that everybody must work, and that full employment will eventually be guaranteed one day. This is the hypocritical discourse of all the candidates in all the elections in the world: they promise jobs. But this is impossible, because work is no longer necessary. This is the simple truth that power is unwilling to say and that we are unable to see.

Instead, when people learn that their work is no longer needed, that migrants and robots can take their jobs, they freak out. They become violent and xenophobic. They vote for a fascist who promises that the Nation will become so powerful that those who belong to it will have the privilege of being salaried slaves all their lives.

The problem is that your job is useless. Your time is no longer needed in the same way that it was during the industrial age. But we are unable to see this simple truth, because we are unable to go beyond the limits of our language. A new division of labor time must urgently be developed. The goal is not to defend the existing composition of labor, but to disentangle the possibility of a new one, to emancipate the general intellect, to liberate the power of science, technology, and art from the limits of our language, from the limits of the superstition of work.

IRONY AND THE LIMIT OF OUR LANGUAGE

"The best lack all conviction," says Yeats. Think of the former German pope, Joseph Ratzinger—Pope Benedict XVI—who came to Rome promising the final establishment of truth. Ratzinger was an intellectual and a supporter of absolute truth. Right-wing Catholics felt emboldened by his ascent to the throne. He said: "God is one, and the Truth is one." In his best-known speech, delivered in Regensburg, Bavaria, the philosopher Ratzinger denounced relativism, which he regarded as the plague of modernity.

I'm not generally a fan of Nanni Moretti, but I like *Habemus Papam*, the movie he directed in 2011. It's a movie about the fragility of human beings—in particular, about the fragility of a human being who is elected pope: Cardinal Melville (played by Michel Piccoli). When he is expected to give his first public speech to a massive crowd assembled in St. Peter's Square, he realizes that he has nothing to say. All of a sudden, he is overwhelmed by the reality of the world, and he mumbles: "I cannot speak." Then he goes to see a psychoanalyst (played by Nanni Moretti). The Pope is depressed because he has seen the truth that he was trying to conceal: that there is no truth in the world. In February 2013, Joseph Ratzinger decided to follow in the footsteps of Michel Piccoli. Ratzinger became the first pope to resign in five centuries.

Today, the relationship between reality and imagination is growing more complicated than Jean Baudrillard could ever have imagined. The real pope imitates the actor impersonating a pope and accepts the dark truth that he is not strong enough to sustain the responsibility of telling the truth, because he feels that the truth is evading him.

Obviously, this is only my interpretation of the resignation of Ratzinger, which was an act of intellectual courage and moral humility. How does one understand the decision of a pope, who has been chosen by God through the intermediary of the Holy Spirit, to resign? I think the only possible interpretation is that Benedict felt depressed, and spoke sincerely with God, and humbly revealed his intimate apocalypse.

Depression is not about guilt, nor is it a limitation of the reasoning mind. It is the disconnection of reasoning from desire. Then, Mario Bergoglio was elected pope, becoming the first Pope Francis in the history of the Catholic Church. He went to the window overlooking St. Peter's Square and said: "*Buonasera.* I'm the man who comes from the end of the world." He meant Argentina, a country ravaged by the beast of financial capitalism. Since that moment, the apocalypse has shone through the acts of Bergoglio, because he is a man who dares to face the end. From the end of the world, Francis has been opening a new path in theology.

Shortly after his election, he gave an interview to the magazine *Civiltà cattolica*. In the interview, he reflects on the three theological virtues: faith, hope, and charity. My interpretation of Bergoglio's remarks is that the main problem for Christians today is not faith. Nor is it truth. Something is more urgent: the focus of Christians today should be charity and mercy. The Church, in the words of Bergoglio, should be thought of as a war hospital.

This is sometimes called "compassion." It is sometimes called "solidarity." Deleuze and Guattari, in the introduction to *What Is Philosophy?*, speak of "friendship." But, what is friendship? It is the ability to create a common world, a world of ironic enunciations and expectations. Friendship is the possibility of creating a common path in the course of time. As the Zapatistas say, quoting the poet Antonio Machado, "*Caminante no hay camino el camino se hace al andar*" (we make the road by walking). There is no truth, there is no meaning, but we can create a bridge beyond the abyss of the nonexistence of truth.

"The best lack all conviction" means that the best have irony, the nonassertive language that aims to tune in to many levels of meaning. The ironic smile also implies empathy, the ability to share the precariousness of life without heaviness. When irony is divorced from empathy, when it loses the lightness and pleasure of precariousness, it turns into cynicism. When irony is divorced from empathy and solidarity, depression takes ahold of the soul.

For semiologists, cynicism and irony are related, because they share the presumption that truth does not exist. But we have to go beyond semiotics: the two concepts differ because the ironic person is someone who does not believe, but rather empathically feels the common ground of understanding. The cynical person is someone who has lost contact with pleasure and who bends to power because power is their only refuge. The cynical person bends to the power of reality, while the ironic person knows that reality is a projection of the mind, of many interwoven minds.

When philosophers realized that God was dead and that there was no metaphysical foundation for our interpretations, different ethical stances emerged. One stance was based on aggressiveness and the violent enforcement of the *Wille zur Macht*: there is no truth in the world, but I'm stronger than you, and my strength is the source of my power which establishes truth. Another stance was irony: friendship and egalitarian sharing can build a bridge of meaning across the abyssal nonexistence of meaning.

BIORHYTHM AND ALGORITHM

Depression can evolve in different ways: if you look at the present reality of America, you see that its prevailing evolution of depression is Donald Trump.

"The worst are full of passionate intensity," says Yeats. Faith in belonging and identity is the fake ground of passionate intensity. Belonging implies a natural ontological or historical ground of conformity between individuals. Therefore, belonging implies violence and submission. If you want to belong, you must accept the rules of conformity. Identity is the result of this process of conformity and subjection. Passionate intensity is the foundation of the identity that humiliated people crave. But identity has to be protected against existence, against transformation, against becoming, against pleasure, because pleasure is dis-identity. Identity is a simulation of belonging that is asserted through violence against the other.

"Surely the second coming is at hand; / ... a vast image out of *Spiritus Mundi* / Troubles my sight." In 1919, Yeats expected the second coming of Jesus Christ. However, in the decade that followed, Hitler came instead. So, we should ask: What is going to happen now? I'll try to reframe the present situation from the point of view of rhythm. In particular, I want to say something about algorithms and biorhythm.

Rhythm is the singularization of time. Rhythm is scanning time in attunement with cosmic breathing. Rhythm is the vibration that aims to harmonize the singularity of breathing and the surrounding chaos. Poetry is the error that leads to new continents of meaning.

Although the theory of biorhythm elaborated by Wilhelm Fliess at the end of the nineteenth century is generally considered pseudoscientific, I'm interested in its metaphorical implications. The organism is composed of vibrant matter, and the pulsations of the organism enter into a rhythmic relationship with the pulsations of other surrounding organisms. The conjunction of conscious and sensitive organisms is a vibrating relationship: individual organisms search for a common rhythm, a common emotional ground of understanding, and this search is a sort of oscillation that results in a possible (or impossible) syntony.

Within the conjunctive sphere of biorhythm, the process of signification and interpretation is a vibrational process. When the process of signification is penetrated by connective machines, it is reformatted. It mutates in a way that implies a reduction: a reduction to the syntactic logic of the algorithm.

The word "algorithm" comes from the name of the Arabic mathematician Al-Khwarizmi (meaning, a native of Khwarazm), whose work introduced sophisticated mathematics to the West. However, I prefer a different etymology and a different meaning. "Algorithm" for me has to do with the Greek word *algos*, meaning pain. Furthermore, the English word "algid" refers to frigidity, both physical and emotional. The pain of the algorithm results from the constriction of the organism, the stiffening of the vibrational agent of enunciation, and the reduction of the continuum of experience to the dictates of computation. When the social concatenation is mediated by connective machines, human agency undergoes a process of reformatting. As Jane Bennett describes:

> No one really knows what human agency is, or what humans are doing when they are said to perform as agents.

> In the face of every analysis, human agency remains something of a mystery. If we do not know just how it is that human agency operates, how can we be so sure that the processes through which nonhumans make their mark are qualitatively different? An assemblage owes its agentic capacity to the vitality of the materialities that constitute it. Something like this congregational agency is called *shi* in Chinese tradition. *Shi* helps to "illuminate something that is usually difficult to capture in discourse: namely, the kind of potential that originates not in human initiative but instead results from the very disposition of things." *Shi* is the style, energy, propensity, trajectory, or élan inherent to a specific arrangement of things. Originally a word used in military strategy, *shi* emerged in the description of a good general who must be able to read and then ride the *shi* of a configuration of moods, winds, historical trends, and armaments: *shi* names the dynamic force emanating from a spatio-temporal configuration rather than from any particular element within it. ... The *shi* of an assemblage is vibratory.[2]

When the algorithm enters the realm of social concatenation, modes of interaction undergo a reformatting process, and algorithmic logic pervades and subjugates the vibrant concatenation. The insertion of the algorithm into the semiotic process breaks the continuum of semiosis and life. In the connective domain, interpretation is reduced to the syntactical recognition of discreet states. The vibrational sign is stiffened, to the point of losing the ability to decode and to interpret ambiguousness and irony. Difference is then interpreted according to the rules of repetition, and the indetermination that makes poetical misunderstanding (or hyper-understanding) possible is canceled. As the semiosphere is reformatted according to the algorithm, the vibratory nature of biorhythm is suffocated. Breathing is banished from the semiotic

[2] Jane Bennett, *Vibrant Matter: A Political Ecology of Things* (Duke University Press, 2010), 34–35.

exchange, and poetry—the error that leads to the discovery of new continents of meaning, the excess that contains new imaginings and new possibilities—is frozen.

THE GESTALT TANGLE AND CHAOS

In nonphilosophical parlance, what I'm speaking about here is our present impotence. Our cognitive activity is captured within the connective syntax, and the general intellect, separated from the social body, expands and produces according to the logic inscribed in the algorithm. The collaboration of millions of cognitive workers worldwide is entangled in the algorithmic form of capitalism: knowledge and technology are directed and contained by the dominant paradigm, the gestalt.

A gestalt is not merely a form; it is a form that generates forms according to the gestalt itself. A particular gestalt gives us the possibility of seeing a certain shape in the surrounding flow of visual impulses. But by the same token, this gestalt forbids us from seeing something else in the same flow of visual impulses. A gestalt is a facilitator of vision and simultaneously a disabler of vision (and generally of perception). Our present political problem can be described in terms of a gestalt of entanglement and disentanglement. How can biorhythm disentangle itself from the algorithm and eventually reprogram the algorithm itself?

In "From Chaos to the Brain," the last chapter of Deleuze and Guattari's *What Is Philosophy?*, they speak about aging. Aging essentially means being invaded by chaos: the aging brain becomes unable to elaborate the surrounding chaos. *Too fast, too fast.* The infosphere around my brain is going too fast for emotional and critical elaboration.

Senescence is a defining feature of our times. People are living longer and reproducing less (with the exception of certain Muslim and African countries). The demographic decline of the white race is an explanation for the mounting wave of reactive supremacism, which is first and foremost an impotent supremacism. Trump won because of this sentiment.

Obama came to the fore proclaiming, "Yes, we can." But the Obama years were marked by impotence. This impotence has fed frustration and rage, ultimately nurturing fascism. Is there a way out of this impotent rage? How can we heal the trauma and go beyond the post-traumatic effects of the present apocalypse?

We must shift the focus of our theoretical attention from the sphere of politics to the sphere of neuroplasticity. We must create technical platforms to enable a neurological reshuffling of the general intellect. I call this perspective the second coming of communism.

THE COMEBACK OF THE EVENT AS TERROR AND DEMENTIA

2018

Humans know the present
only the gods have knowledge of the future
wise men instead can perceive imminent things
but they are so busy reading the books
that their hearing is deranged so
they confusedly catch the echo
of what is coming, and devoutly
listen to it. Outside, in the streets
the crowds are completely unaware
of what is going to happen to them.

—Konstantinos Petrou Kavafis,
"Σοφοί δε Προσιόντων"[1]

The most venerated oracle of the ancient world was in Delphi. The high priestess in charge of the oracle was named Pythia. This name is derived from *Pytho*, which, in mythology, was the original name of Delphi. The Greeks derived the name of this place from the verb πύθειν (*púthein*, "to rot"). πύθειν refers to the sickly sweet smell of the monstrous Python's decomposing body after she was slain by Apollo. Pythia was punk. Punk is the decomposition in which we can find the only truth of life.

Prophecy is based on smelling rot and is expressed in words that do not have an unequivocal meaning, but rather open a range of possible interpretations. Prophecy is thus an enigma. While the secret of a prophecy refers to a hidden truth that may eventually be brought to light, the enigma refers to unresolvable ambiguousness and demands infinite interpretation.

Psychomancy (*psycho-manteia*) is the investigation of the futures that are taking shape in the social mind: a psycho-social form of divination based on the interpretation of ambiguous signs proceeding from the psychosphere.

The task of the oracle, at this point, is not to predict the apocalypse: the apocalypse is already taking place. Rather, a contemporary

1. Constantino Kavafis, *La Poesie*, ed. Nicola Crocetti (Torino: Giulio Einaudi editore, 2015), my translation.

oracle's job is to divine how we must come to terms with the apocalypse as it unfolds.

SIMULACRUM AND BIO-INFO DESTINY

The philosophical adventure of Jean Baudrillard can be viewed in relation to three successive moments in late modern history: the age of consciousness, when the students of the world rose together to fulfil the promises of Reason; the age of the market, when events were frozen into simulation; and the age of the brainless body, the age of revenge and mental darkening.

Beginning in 1966, the young Baudrillard was involved with the intellectual group Utopie, along with Henri Lefebvre, Hubert Tonka, and others. Baudrillard was deeply influenced by the Situationist critique of the spectacle. The concept of the spectacle, however, was charged with late-Hegelian implications. In fact, according to Guy Debord, the spectacle is the mirror of our alienation, a condition of inauthentic experience.

The revolutionary project of 1968 was intended to restore authenticity of life thanks to the reversal and the overcoming of the spectacular conditions of capital, consumption, and advertising. When the political euphoria of the rebellion faded in the following years, Baudrillard abandoned the conceptual frames of the spectacle and alienation, acknowledging the inescapability of the new stage of capitalism based on the simulacrum. If the spectacle is the mirror of our alienation, the simulacrum is the replacement of reality with a replicable projection, and the pre-emption of events, acts of creative singularity. The simulacrum is a copy that has no original. It is the projection of the technology of reproduction, and it cannot be reversed, because its source is beyond our reach and because we only exist inside it.

In the 1980s, when Thatcher asserted the neoliberal faith in the God called the market, when Wozniak and Jobs designed connective architectures, simulation emerged as the dominant form in the sphere of cultural experience: digital technology, networked connection, genetic biotechnology, and neoliberal revolution are the steps which mark the transition from the sphere of history to the sphere of generation.

The modern mind was enshrined in the intentionality of the project: the ontological freedom of humans, the political potency of will, the imaginative creation of the future. This mental attitude turns out to be ineffective and impotent as we enter into the domain of generation. The word "generation" refers to the replication of information in recombinable units: info-generation (algorithm, big data interfaced with artificial-intelligence devices) and bio-genetics (replication and engineering of the DNA) now tend to replace the intentionality of human acts.

THE PROPHECY OF BAUDRILLARD

In *Symbolic Exchange and Death*, Baudrillard outlines the impending world of postmodernity from the point of view of a general disappearance. He writes: "The finalities have disappeared; we are now engendered by models."[2] This change marks a key shift: beyond this point, the conceptual framework of modernity starts dissolving, and a new framework emerges. The figure looming on the horizon of Baudrillard's 1976 book is the bio-info automaton. Since that moment, we know that the proliferation of AI into social-cognitive structures has enabled the slow replacement of the living brain with techno-linguistic automatisms, for example.

The word "prophecy" signals the interpretation of what is present, what is in front of you. The prophet says what is already here, like Federico Campagna explains in the book *Prophetic Culture: Recreation for Adolescents*.[3] The prophet is an interpreter of maladies. Thus, interpretation is the perception of the symptoms as tendencies, as signs of emerging mutations, and of new Events.

2. Jean Baudrillard, *Symbolic Exchange and Death*, trans. Iain Hamilton Grant (Thousand Oaks, CA: Sage Publications, 1993), 9.
3. Federico Campagna, *Prophetic Culture: Recreation for Adolescents* (London: Bloomsbury, 2021).

In this sense, Baudrillard was prophetic, but the paradox of his prophecy is that he predicts that the prophecy will die. Indeed, his words can be read as a meta-prophecy: a prophecy about the disappearance of the prophecy.

Thus, his style is based on two rhetorical tricks: the nostalgic "no longer" and the assertive "will not happen".

Among the infinite number of events preempted by the info-generative simulation, the end is the main victim. Everything is destined to return forever as replication, so nothing can be terminated, and no excitement can lead to orgasm.
In his later book *The Illusion of the End* (1992), Baudrillard writes: "Just as physicists now see their particles only as a trajectory on a screen, we no longer have the pulsing of events, but only the cardiogram."[4] Here, we see that what haunts Baudrillard is the end of the event of the end.

By the '80s, when he wrote *America* and *The Transparency of Evil*, the end became the asymptotic horizon of his vision. It's viewed as the unfulfilled promise, the imminent possibility that is never actualized, because the logic of replicant generation makes the event of the end an asymptote. The procedure of recombination turns the event of the end into something that is always approaching, an unreachable point of orgasmic discharge.

INSCRIPTION/PRESCRIPTION

Baudrillard's other rhetorical trick is the paradoxical de-negation or disaffirmation, made most evident in his famous lines: "the gulf war did not take place" and "the year 2000 will not take place." In the hyper-reality produced by the recombinant machine of digital technology, events do not occur. Rather, only the simulated effects of info-bio generation are allowed to access the space of the real. Thus, the real becomes a desert, the pre-conceived projection of an abstraction. This prophetic style again turns prophecy into

4. Jean Baudrillard, *The Illusion of the End*, trans. Chris Turner (Stanford, CA: Stanford University Press, 1994), 19.

something quite strange. It's as if his predication is to say that the prophecy will no longer be possible. The predication generates the future.

Events in general have been canceled because finalities have been replaced by code. Reality has been cleansed, smoothed, and finally digitized. Hyper-reality indeed. In his 2000 *The Vital Illusion*, he continues this train of thought: "Cleansing is the prime activity of this fin de siècle—the laundering of a dirty history, of dirty money, of corrupt consciousness, of the polluted planet—the cleansing of memory."[5] Let's not forget that the '90s was the decade of the Yugoslavian Civil War, the setting for the comeback of the Nazi principle of ethnic homogeneity pursued by the nation-state on the European stage. This was also the decade when computational recombination penetrated the collective brain and the social body.

For Baudrillard, as prediction is replaced by the prescriptive action of the code, data are inscribed into the future, and the future becomes replication of the abstract eternity of computation. The imagination of the future is thus captured by ubiquitous devices of translation: the algorithmic enforcement of the eternity of capital.

THE COMEBACK OF THE EVENT

In the third phase of his life, Baudrillard was confronted with the event as apocalypse. September 11, 2001, marked the return of the unpredictable to the scene of world history. In his book *America*, published in 1985, he had described the newly built towers of Manhattan as the symbol of digitalization, of binary replication. The infinite potency of the simulacrum was visibly embedded in them. On that 2001 Tuesday morning, however, that symbol of the omnipotence of the binary code was destroyed. In other words, the unthinkable happened: the unpredicted event was back. In *The Spirit of Terrorism*, a small book that widely circulated in the

5. Jean Baudrillard, *The Vital Illusion*, (New York: Columbia University Press, 2000), 33.

aftermath of the attacks, Baudrillard speaks as if with a sense of relief: "The fact that we have dreamt of this event, that everyone without exception has dreamt of it—because no one can avoid dreaming of the destruction of any power that is hegemonic to this degree—is unacceptable to the Western moral conscience."[6]

Our moral consciousness rebels against mass killing, but our unconsciousness rejoices. Revenge surfaces at the horizon of the new century. In response to Fukuyama's predication of the end of history with the collapse of the Soviet Union, Baudrillard retorts: "'it was possible to see this as a resurrection of history beyond its proclaimed end."[7]

But, in truth, History did not reappear as the conscious implementation of universal Reason. Rather, it returned in the form of the violent enforcing of identitarian particularity. Chaos jeopardized the automaton, and so the automaton tried to reclaim control. The comeback of the Event, of History, takes the shape of terror and of dementia.

As human intelligence is overpowered by AI, consciousness is replaced by the adaptation of the individual brain to the almighty automaton.

Unfortunately, (for us, but perhaps luckily for him), Jean Baudrillard died in the very moment in which Hell emerged as the horizon of our time: Trump, Brexit, Bolsonaro, all symptoms of the age of dementia and terror that probably will never end.

6. Jean Baudrillard, *The Spirit of Terrorism*, trans. Chris Turner (London: Verso, 2002), 5.
7. Baudrillard, *The Spirit of Terrorism*, 28.

GENERAL INTELLECT AND THE TERMINATION MACHINE

2018

In the 1960s, technological innovation and social consciousness converged and reached their high points in the explosion of labor and student rebellions. While May 1968 in Paris is better known internationally, in Italy the year 1969 saw massive worker and student rebellions, known as Italy's "Hot Autumn." As some say, in Italy, 1968 lasted for ten years. Since then, the potency of technical tools and machines has steadily expanded, technology has grown more and more pervasive, while social consciousness has been receding. As a result, technique has been enhancing its grip over social life, while society has been losing control of technology and therefore has grown less and less able to govern itself.

During the conjuncture that is called 1968, social consciousness was expected to preside over technological change and to direct it toward the common good. But, as is now clear, the contrary occurred. When a new technological horizon appeared, following the diffusion of electronics and computing, established leftist parties and mass labor unions regarded the technological change as a danger, rather than as an opportunity for popular mastery. Consequently, liberation from labor was labeled unemployment, and the Left wasted its energies countering the unstoppable technical transformation. What interests me here is the relation between information and consciousness evidenced by that response. I define information as knowledge objectified in signs that is conveyed by media. Consciousness, rather, is the subjective elaboration and the singularization of the contents of knowledge.

After '68, and particularly in the wake of the digital acceleration of the infosphere, simultaneous to the neoliberal turn, the sphere of objectified knowledge did expand enormously, while the available time for conscious elaboration shrunk. This double dynamic provoked a reshaping of social consciousness: the relative reduction of available time has resulted in a systemic downsizing of the individual conscious assimilation of information and the singularization of knowledge. In other words, the rhythm of technological innovation has intensified, while social awareness has simultaneously decreased.

1968 is also the year of *2001: A Space Odyssey*. Stanley Kubrick's vision seems to have anticipated the present confrontation between artificial intelligence and humankind. The movie evokes the central question implicit in the discourse of '68: the relation between human labor and the machine that, in the third decade of this century, is epitomized in the relation between the human mind and AI. Today, we have built a cognitive machine that is emerging as a powerful and tendentially autonomous automaton. The concept of the automaton refers to concatenations that incorporate human decisions in their technical infrastructures; for example, the techno-financial system is a super-organism that is able to subsume human will. Similarly, the military system is a super-organism that integrates human passions and technical tools into the dynamics of deadly competition. And the internet—which in '60s counterculture was imagined as a tool for liberation and the expansion of popular culture—has proven to be a sphere for the proliferation of ever-expanding alienation. Like the techno-financial system and the military system, AI has given birth to an ungovernable automaton.

We are left to wonder if the mission of the automaton is to emancipate humans from exploitation, or to increase exploitation; to elevate the quality of life, or to terminate humankind. While AI is expanding in the technical sphere, human ignorance has increased in relative terms. Thus, demented behavior becomes more pronounced: mass support for racism, nationalism, and religious fanaticism are the other sides of the automation of intelligence. The separation of the automated brain from the living body results in the expanding dementia of the brainless social body.

On December 2, 1964, in Berkeley, Mario Savio gave a speech that can be read as the conscious beginning of the movement of the general intellect against the capitalist exploitation of knowledge.

> There's a time when the operation of the machine becomes so odious, makes you so sick at heart, that you can't take part; you can't even passively take part! And you've got to put your bodies upon the gears and upon the wheels, upon the levers, upon all the apparatus, and you've got to make it stop! And you've got to indicate to the people who run it, to the people who own it, that unless you're free, the machine will be prevented from working at all![1]

Hans-Jürgen Krahl, a thinker and activist from the German '68, argued that a new composition of labor was emerging at the time, due to the insertion of science and technology into the cycles of production and to the emerging consciousness of techno-scientific intelligence, interpreted as a social force.[2] In fact, the prior decade marked the high point in the history of mass education: universal access to the public system of education was an effect of the progressive struggles of the workers' movement.

Critical thought, which had been the exclusive privilege of the bourgeoisie in past centuries, quickly turned into a common good available to most of society. Simultaneously, in those years, the evolution of technology prepared the conditions for the formation of the general intellect, which Marx had conceptualized in the *Grundrisse*. In the "Fragment on Machines," Marx asserts that machines, as a product of knowledge, reduce necessary labor time up to the point of making the emancipation of society from the slavery of salaried labor possible.

In the late 1960s, attempts to form alliances between students and industrial workers could be interpreted as acts of ideological or moral solidarity. In fact, students were the bearers of the force of knowledge, while workers were expressing a widespread refusal of salaried exploitation. The political alliance between them implied the prospect of an organized process of reduction of labor time. In Italy the slogan "*lavorare tutti lavorare meno*" (everyone at work so everyone can work less) was the culmination of those years of social mobilization. But this alliance did not last long, because the political leadership of the workers' movement proved unable to transform technology into an opportunity. They saw technology as dangerous, and they engaged in the losing strategy of defending jobs rather than in the strategy of taking control of developing technology to reduce work time.

1. "'The Bodies upon the Gears': Mario Savio's Speech on the Sproul Hall Steps, UC-Berkeley," in Jim Willis, *1960s Counterculture: Documents Decoded* (Santa Barbara, CA: ABC-CLIO, 2015).
2. Hans-Jürgen Krahl, "Thesen zum allgemeinen Verhältnis von wissenschaftlicher Intelligenz und proletarischem Klassenbewusstsein," in *Konstitution und Klassenkampf* (Frankfurt: Verlag Neue Kritik, 1971).

During the last few decades, the main subject of my research has been the question of which forms of subjectivation of cognitive labor are possible in the age of semiocapitalism? With the rise of corporate artificial intelligence, I see a turning point: social subjectivity has been dispossessed of intelligence and has been invaded by dementia. Cognitive workers have been subjected to the rule of capitalist competition and are obliged to build self-learning machines in conditions of pervasive war. We are now facing the final dilemma: should we stop the automaton before it terminates humanity?

According to Martin Wolf:

> Humanity is Doctor Faustus. It, too, seeks knowledge and power and is prepared to make almost any bargain to achieve it, regardless of consequences. Even worse, it is a species of competing Doctor Faustuses, who seek knowledge and power, as he did. We have been experiencing the impact of the social media revolution on our society and politics. Some warn of its consequences for our children. But we cannot halt the bargains we have made. We will not halt this revolution either. We are Faustus. We are Mephistopheles. The AI revolution will roll on.[3]

We have built an entity whose mission is computational order. We have given this entity autonomy and the ability to redefine its procedures and its conclusions. This machine is going to implement order at all costs. This is why we have programmed it. The only obstacle to the full realization of order, the only chaotic factor, is humanity. Therefore, the word "extinction" takes on its full meaning in the contemporary context: automated termination.

3. Martin Wolff, "The Threat and Promise of Artificial Intelligence," *Financial Times*, May 9, 2023.

(SENSITIVE) CONSCIOUSNESS AND TIME:
Against the Transhumanist Utopia

2019

HEGEL AND LEIBNIZ

Two pan-logical projects tower above the history of modernity: the recombinant project of Leibniz and the teleological project of Hegel. In Leibniz, the world is preordained as a computational program, while in Hegel, the order of the world is the final result of historical conflicts that pave the way for the realization of the Absolute Spirit.

But as Baudrillard writes in *Symbolic Exchange and Death*: “Finalities have disappeared, models are generating us.”[1] So, at the end of modernity, the historical project of Hegel has collapsed and now lies torn apart in the chaotic geo-scape of the postmodern century.

Simultaneously, at the intersection of biotechnology and artificial intelligence, a transhumanist utopia is emerging as a Leibnizian dream (or nightmare): the reduction of the human world to computation, the prescriptive potency of a recombinant computational god. The transhumanist utopia feeds on the rotting of humanism and on the current catastrophe of critical reason that Yuval Harari outlines as a dissociation of intelligence and consciousness.

As I know that the word “consciousness” is gravid with spiritualist and idealist abuse, I have decided to replace this word with “sensibility,” in order to define the kind of mental activity that cannot be reduced to computation or biological determinism. In this sense, consciousness implies sensibility.

CHAOS AND THE AUTOMATON

Two actors emerge on the stage of the imminent: artificial intelligence and natural dementia. When we speak of new technologies converging toward the implementation of cognitive automaton, we should not forget that this process develops amid spreading psychosis and identitarian obsession.

1. Jean Baudrillard, *Symbolic Exchange and Death* (Thousand Oaks, CA: Sage Publications, 1993), 9.

Inorganic intelligence, incorporated into social life through a network of techno-linguistic info-devices, is governed and applied by a demented social organism: artificial intelligence in the hands of the ferocious stupidity that prevails on the political stage. The self-building automaton emerges in the context of global chaos, and, in the process, sensibility is separated from intelligence. The sensitive organism does not comply with the computational perfection of the automaton.

Artificial intelligence and social dementia coalesce in the imminent scene.

TECHNO-TOTALITARIAN REICH

The shame and disgust of being human (of having human bodies, and bodily minds) is the psycho-epistemic premise of transhumanist ideology. From Baudelaire to Huysmans to Bataille to Houellebecq, repugnance towards the sexual body (especially relevant in French literary culture) meets California techno-culture and gives birth to the transhumanist eternity of the frozen extra-bodily techno-brain.

Ray Kurzweil argues that the miniaturization of computers will result in nanobots that can enter and repair the human body. Human life could thereby be prolonged to the stage where it would become possible to download the human brain onto a computer, making humans immortal. I do not know if this project (recalling Marvin Minsky and his idea that minds are simply what brains do) is technologically well-founded (I don't think so), but that's not my point here. My point is that this technological project is based on a misunderstanding of the meaning of "human."

Kurzweil writes:

> The power (price-performance, speed, capacity, and bandwidth) of information technologies is growing exponentially at an even faster pace, now doubling about every year ... Human brain scanning is one of these exponentially improving technologies ... Nonbiological intelligence

> will be able to download skills and knowledge from other machines, eventually also from humans ... We will be able to reengineer all of the organs and systems in our biological bodies and brains to be vastly more capable ... Nanobots will have myriad roles within the human body, including reversing human aging (to the extent that this task will not already have been completed through biotechnology, such as genetic engineering).[2]

Following the Cartesian road, transhumanist thinkers take a dualistic approach to the mind-body problem, and assume that the human mind can exist, independently from the body, in a computer.

What is interesting in this dystopian utopia is not the technological anticipation (which may or may not be true), but the political and philosophical implications. The transhumanist vision is based on the reducibility of conscious life to artificial intelligence: this techno-determinism outlines the prospect of a techno-totalitarian empire that obviously reminds one of the German experiment in producing an *Übermensch* civilization. I want to abstain from any ethical or political scandal on this point: I do not consider Nazism the absolute evil, just a particular example of the cruelty of history. My only focus here is the philosophical coherence of the techno-determinist view, regardless of its ethico-political outcome.

In 1958, Günther Anders wrote:

> We can expect that the horrors of the Reich to come will vastly eclipse the horrors of yesterday's Reich. Doubtless, when one day our children or grandchildren, proud of their perfect "co-mechanization," look down from the great heights of their thousand-year reich at yesterday's empire, at the so-called "third" Reich, it will seem to them merely a minor, provincial experiment; one which, in spite of its enormous effort to spread itself everywhere ("tomorrow

2. Ray Kurzweil, *The Singularity Is Near: When Humans Transcend Biology* (New York: Viking Books, 2005), 25, 28.

> the whole world," they said), and its cynical extermination of everything it could not use, was nevertheless unable to remain standing. And doubtless, they will see what happened there as simply a dress rehearsal for totalitarianism, adorned with a foolish ideology, into which world history had ventured prematurely . . .
>
> A new age began on August 6, 1945: the age in which we are able at any moment to transform any location, in fact the entire planet, into a Hiroshima. Ever since this day we have become *modo negativo* almighty. However, since we can now be exterminated at any moment, this also means that since this day we have become totally powerless. No matter how long it takes, even if it lasts an eternity, this age will be the last. This is because its *differentia spezifica*—the possibility of our self-extermination—can never end, unless it be through this end itself.[3]

It is time to fully understand the core of Anders's argument: Nazism should not be seen (only) as a traditionalist and reactionary movement, but also (and mostly) as a cult of functionality, the anticipation of the functional potency of the automaton. The implementation of transhuman entities that can perform inhuman tasks without the participation of humans: this is the perfection of Nazism. The absolute priority of the functional, the rebuilding of the social world based on the principle of economic functionality. The world we are going to irreversibly inhabit.

3. Günther Anders, *Die Atomare Drohung: Radikale Überlegungen zum atomaren Zeitalter* (Munich: C.H. Beck, 2003), 93, my translation.

COLLAPSE OF EURO-CENTERED HUMANISM

The new technologies of the twenty-first century may reverse the humanist revolution, stripping humans of their authority, and empowering non-human algorithms instead.[4]

In "What Begins After the End of the Enlightenment?," Yuk Hui remarks that the thread linking humanism to the Enlightenment is:

> [T]he full realization of a single global axis of time in which all historical times converge into the synchronizing metric of European modernity. It is the moment of disorientation—a loss of direction as well as of the Orient in relation to the Occident. The unhappy consciousness of fascism and xenophobia arises from this inability to orient: as a response, it offers an easy identity politics and an aestheticized politics of technology.[5]

The process of digital globalization has broken this synchronizing metric of European modernity and the cultural supremacy of West-centered Reason; we dwell in the aftermath of this cultural collapse. Because of connective mutation, and because of the psychotic explosion of the unconscious of the media-enhanced social mind, the anthropological dimension that the modern age identified as "human" is dissolving.

The crucial effect of this mutation is the dissociation of consciousness (sensibility) and intelligence in the cognitive activity of the social brain.

4. Yuval Harari, *Homo Deus: A Brief History of Tomorrow* (New York: Penguin Random House, 2015), 397.
5. Yuk Hui, "What Begins After the End of the Enlightenment?," *e-flux journal* 96 (January 2019).

DECOUPLING, DIVERGENCE

In economics and war, intelligence is mandatory: if you want to survive, if you want to beat the competition, you need to be more intelligent than your competitor. Consciousness is superfluous, and even detrimental in many cases. The less intelligence is limited and slowed by sensibility, the more it can pursue automatic goals. The more intelligence is free from the limitations and ambiguity of sensibility, the more an intelligent organism will be effective in the struggle for survival and supremacy.

The transhumanist project is based on the premise that technology is going to enable a perfect simulation of intelligent life. The tacit implication of this project, however, is that intelligent life can be decoupled from sensibility, because from the point of view of the evolutionary economy, sensibility is an unnecessary residual quality, a factor of slowness and inexactness.

The history of social civilization in the last two centuries can be read as an attempt to escape the inflexible law of the survival of the fittest. Social solidarity has been the attempt to transform the world into an anti-natural place of mitigated competition. The autonomy of politics and ethics from the natural law of evolution was based on the conscious limiting of the power of intelligence. When intelligence is not restrained by sensibility, it deploys as brutal force.

The ontological autonomy of human knowledge and human action is the core of the humanist breakthrough. Simultaneously, however, modernity has asserted the economic criterion of evaluation and has reduced knowledge to the economic principle of competition for survival: effectiveness as power.

Modernity, in fact, is the sphere of permanent conflict between the Christian principle of compassion and the Darwinist principle of survival of the fittest. If we wonder who is the fittest, the answer is unequivocal: the fittest is the organism that deploys the strength of intelligence without the limitations of sensibility.

The social meaning of democracy results in an attempt to shelter human life from the supposed laws of Darwin: this attempt has been successful up to a certain point, as long as intelligence and sensibility were combined. This convergence reached its high point in May 1968; then it broke down, and sensibility started to diverge from intelligence.

As democracy has submitted to financial capitalism, and solidarity has been overwhelmed by competition, social civilization has been dismantled and the law of competition has taken the upper hand in the daily business of life.

So, the subjection of technology to capitalist competition has paradoxically paved the way for the comeback of Nature: the principle of natural selection. The philosophical core of Darwinist science has broken the restraints and shelters built by the autonomy of ethico-political action.

Nature is back, and technology is the gizmo that facilitates this return. The earth separates from the World.

EX-PERIENCE, DURATION, AND DEATH

> In the past there were many things that only humans could do. But now robots and computers are catching up and may soon outperform humans in most tasks ... Humans are in danger of losing their economic value, because intelligence is decoupling from sensibility.
>
> So far high intelligence always went hand in hand with a developed consciousness. Only conscious beings could perform tasks that requested a lot of intelligence, such as playing chess, driving cars, diagnosing diseases or identifying terrorists.[6]

At this point, we need to define the meaning of the words "intelligence" and "consciousness."

My definitions are the following: intelligence is the ability to make decisions about decidable alternatives. Consciousness is the ability to decide about undecidable alternatives. Intelligence implies

6. Harari, 361.

computation and combination, while consciousness implies sensibility (aesthetic and erotic) and ethical judgment.

That being said, this answer is too cursory. First, we must understand the implications of the concept of intelligence, starting from Leibnizian computational ontology, from the conceptual distinction between the discrete and the continuous in the transmission of information and in the evolution of life.

By the term "discrete," in opposition to "continuum," we refer to individual entities that can be reduced to finite information. By the term "continuum," on the other hand, we refer to the flow of experience that cannot be reduced to information. The flow of experience is essentially the self-perception of the becoming-other of the sensitive organism. Sensibility detects the infinite variations of becoming in time, as it is based on the self-perception of an organism whose existence is in time. The etymology of the word "experience" implies death: *ex-perire*. Therefore, the conscious organism perceives reality as becoming-other against the background of the destiny of the expiration of the conscious and sensitive organism.

Modern philosophy, since Descartes, has based the self on the *cogito*, so certainty is based on intellection. This Cartesian reduction of the self to the intellectual ability of the mind has blurred the border between intelligence and consciousness.

Reason is a projection of measure, a reduction of the world to what is measurable in discrete terms. This reduction of the self to reason as the ability to measure lies at the origin of the late-modern catastrophe (Adorno and Horkheimer recognized this point in the preface to the *Dialectic of Enlightenment*).

Descartes finds proof for the existence of the "self" in the unquestionable existence of thought, but it is more useful and more comprehensive to find the foundation of the self in sensibility: I *feel*, therefore I am.

But self-perception has no logical meaning, nor is it measurable or reducible to discrete minimal units. There is no measurement for self-perception, as self-perception happens in the sphere of the infinitely divisible—that is, in the sphere of the continuum.

Existence does not correspond to reason. Only sensibility allows for an integration of intellection and judgment (ethical judgment, and, in the end, aesthetic judgment).

TIME AND TEMPORALITY

Assuming the infinite divisibility of physical matter, Leibniz is aware of the duplicity of matter in time. It is simultaneously "actual discrete divided infinitely" and a continuum of experience.[7]

The continuity of experience is the perception of the continuum, a flow that deploys through time—or rather emanates through time as duration. The continuity of an aggregate of extensive discrete states is intensive. This is consciousness as sensibility—the intensive elaboration of the extended world. Extended realities draw their perceptual consistency and their experiential continuity from the intensive vibration of becoming in time.
This means that death, the ultimate destination of time, is the source of the intensity.

As Carlo Rovelli writes, "Quantum theory does not describe things as they evolve in time, but it describes how things are evolving in mutual relation."[8]

Since the time of Zeno and the tortoise, the problem of the infinite divisibility of matter (and of time) has been crucial. To define the relation between intelligence and consciousness, let's say that intelligence is the ability to acknowledge an aggregate as a combination of discrete units (i.e., the ability to compute a temporal extension in terms of discrete units of conventional time). Consciousness as sensibility, on the other hand, is the ability to experience the continuous quality of matter and of temporality.

7. Gottfried Wilhelm Leibniz, letter to Burchard de Volder, referenced in Stefano Mugnai, *Introduzione alla filosofia di Leibniz* (Turin: Einaudi, 2001), 114, my translation.
8. Carlo Rovelli, *L'ordine del tempo* (Milan: Adelphi, 2017), my translation.

In *Durée et Simultanéité*, Henri Bergson writes:

> We cannot speak of reality as duration without introducing consciousness ... The mathematical person will not take notice of it, because rightly she is interested in the measure of things, not in their nature ... Duration is essentially the protraction of something that exists no more into something that does exist.[9]

Mental activity is indissociable from the perception of time, from the subconscious awareness of body-mind decomposition: the subconscious of death, inasmuch as death means becoming other to the conscious sensitive organism. Therefore, we can define consciousness as the cognitive implication of death.

Bergson distinguishes computational time, objectified in clocks and in the economic value of goods, from lived temporality (*temps vécu*), a duration that is not reducible to computation.

Computational time is the subject of mathematics and economics, but society lives in the incomputable time of death as destination (not as destiny). Ethics and aesthetics are suited to think this incomputable time. But ethical and aesthetic judgments have little to do with intelligence, and nothing to do with certainty and truth.

Transhumanism is an ideology that mistakes computation for existence, and, therefore, it is a philosophical deception. It is the other face of the inhuman dementia that grows in the shadow of the forced computabilization of the incomputable. Here we should start to reflect on extinction, on death as the condition for the perception of time, and on consciousness as the vibrational situatedness of the self.

9. Henri Bergson, *Durée et Simultaneité* (Paris: Presse Universitaire de France, 1922), 48.

Rovelli again:

> Fear of death seems to me as an error of evolution: many animals have an instinctive faculty of terror and escape if a predator approaches. It's a healthy reaction, as it allows them to avoid danger. But selection has generated hairless apes with hypertrophic frontal lobes who have an excessive ability to predict the future. This is a helpful privilege, but the risk is that we permanently see the inevitability of death, thus igniting persistent terror and a need to escape.
>
> Hence, I think that the fear of death is an accidental and silly disturbance that blends together two independent evolutionary pressures: a product of bad automatic connections in our brain. Everything has a limited time of existence. Including the human race.[10]

10. Rovelli, *L'ordine del tempo*, my translation.

DESIRE, PLEASURE, SENILITY, AND EVOLUTION

2020

Energy is eternal delight.

—William Blake

This essay is short and inconsistent. It grew out of a talk I gave at a conference titled Art After Culture at e-flux in New York in June 2019. When I was invited to speak, the subject I proposed was: “Desire, Pleasure, Evolution.” I will begin with a few things about those topics, but will move on to other things—namely, senility and evolution.

So, desire and pleasure. I recently discovered that somewhere—I don’t remember exactly where—Gilles Deleuze recounts one of his exchanges with Michel Foucault. Before leaving Deleuze’s house, Foucault kindly and shyly, in his style, remarks to Deleuze: you know, I must confess to you that the word “desire” disgusts me. I would prefer to use the word “pleasure.” Would you agree?

Deleuze, however, does not agree at all. He absolutely disdains the word “pleasure.” Actually, in a lecture he delivered in Vincennes in 1973, Deleuze said something along the lines of: *Plaisir, quel horrible et atroce mot. Qu’est-ce que ça signifie? Le décharge?* (Pleasure, what a horrible, atrocious word. What does it mean? Discharge?)

This discussion between the two reveals a dimension of desire as discussed by Deleuze and Félix Guattari that has always escaped me. During my years in Paris in the late ’70s, I first came to realize that desire is the engine that mobilizes social energies, but I did not consider at all the distinction between desire and pleasure. It wasn’t until last year that I understood the difference, while I was reading about that exchange between Deleuze and Foucault.

Of course, one can find an explication of the difference in Jean Baudrillard, the real wise man of the Parisian scene of the ’70s and ’80s. Baudrillard says: desire, sure, we all desire beautiful things, but beware that the entire history of capitalism is based on permanent desire.

Now, in my old age I have come to (painfully) appreciate the difference between desire and pleasure, and I understand that capitalism is, in fact, based on an endless postponement of pleasure, and simultaneously on the permanent excitement of desire. Virtual capitalism—what I call semiocapitalism—is an intensification of both these conditions, postponing pleasure and exciting desire.

Another catalyst for my realization of how they differ is feeling physically, personally, that growing old essentially means losing the ability to access certain spheres of pleasure, while desire continues undisturbed. Beyond my personal experience, and its suggestion of a larger condition, there is something more interesting, and more disturbing, in the relationship between the two. This relationship—between the permanent burning of desire and the inaccessibility, the unattainability, of pleasure—has something to do with the present historical moment of transition, the present step in human evolution.

Why are older people so nervous? *Cantankerous*, even? I don't even know the meaning of this word, but it sounds right. Why are old people so malignant?

I have two answers. The first has to do with the disappearance of neurons and synapses in old age: the reduction in the ability to process information, the loss of subtlety, the loss of definition in the relationship between sensibility and experience. The second is that we—we humans, old humans in particular—tend to cling to life because we think it is our private property. *This life is mine, and I don't want to lose this property.*

The denial of death is deeply inscribed in the modern mind. As the world's white population grows old, this has provoked something resembling a social psychosis, an aggressive grasping among the old for all that is left: naked life, putrescent life.

At the end of his beautiful book *The Order of Time*, Carlo Rovelli writes that the fear of death is a mistake of evolution. It is an error provoked by the inability to think the world without one's own presence within it, an inability to think the world *without me*. Modern culture emphasizes the individual in continuous competition with other individuals and consequently erases a sense of community among people. Thus, it has turned death into something that cannot be thought, said, or psychically elaborated. Death is systematically denied, which in turn leaves the individual alone in an infinite desert of sadness, and ultimately unable to see the continuity among the individual and the community, among me and you.

Furthermore, modern capitalism is based on an idolatry of energy. It is based on an obsession with growth, expansion, productivity, acceleration—futurist obsessions that have made senility unthinkable.

Why am I writing about these strange and slightly scary subjects? Why am I talking about senility and death? Of course, the main reason is that they are my problems. But, believe me, they're not my problems alone. They are two of the main problems of humankind in the present. The denial of death, linked to the idolatry of energy and expansion, has turned decline and un-growth into purely negative tendencies and frugality into scarcity. So, in this sense, life has become a paranoid fight against the passage of time.

I strongly believe that senescence is the (unseen or unfathomed) key to understanding the present historical conundrum, just as decline is simultaneously the problem and the solution to the late-modern crisis.

Firstly, we can surmise that this situation is to do with demographic reasons. Senility now tends to be the condition of most of the Western population, and not only of the Western population. While the African population grows exponentially, while the populations in the Middle East and on the Indian subcontinent steadily grow, Western dominators and aggressors are ageing, they are losing energy, and, most of all, they are losing the innocent faith in the future that belongs most to younger people.

The demographic gap between the population explosion in much of the South and the decline in the North is probably one of the central reasons for contemporary racism and aggressiveness. Old people have transferred their declining potency to the machines, and the war machine is in motion as a permanent menace against those oppressed in the South, the colonized people who try to migrate towards the declining Northern lands. This is why we must consider the crucial problem of senility if we want to understand anything at all about what is happening in the social, cultural, and political spheres.

Let's think about the worldwide resurgence of "fascism." Donald Trump, Matteo Salvini, Boris Johnson, Nigel Farage,

Vladimir Putin, and Recep Erdoğan. Are they fascists? No, they are not. And the process that is expanding in large parts of the world, is this fascism? No, it is not.

Fascism was a historic phenomenon comprised of young people. It was a movement based on the will-to-power of a strong, energetic, futuristic movement. It involved people who expected a bright future, and promoted expansion, the colonization of territories and markets. Nobody expects a bright future nowadays. And expansion is no longer possible, because the entire planet is subjugated, while markets are saturated. The colonization of territorial spaces is over—only time can be colonized nowadays. The only direction for expansion today is the intensification of time and the acceleration of mental rhythms. Only the virtual expansion of cognitive space and the accelerated circulation of signs is possible. But this kind of intensification is blowing up the nervous systems of humankind.

Forty years ago, I remember shouting with some young British musicians, "No future! No future!" I thought it was the provocation of an unlikely avant-garde. Now, everybody thinks that the future is over; now, the sentiment aligns with a conformist position held by most of humankind. "No future" has become common sense, and this is why cynicism is expanding in contemporary culture, in contemporary political behavior. Futurism was the expression of a society that expected something from the future and of a society that truly felt the warmth of community, whether encapsulated in the nation, the family, or social ties to working communities. All the above was the reality of lived experience a hundred years ago. No more! Today, the nation is a nonexistent thing. The dissolution of the nation is an effect of the pervasive digitalization of information and of power based on information. Do you think that Google belongs to the United States? Not at all. The United States belongs to the territory of Google. So does Italy, and France, and so on.

National sovereignty has been dissolved by the virtual ubiquity of power; the nation has come back as a myth, as an aggressive form of identification, as nostalgic rage.

Belonging has been transformed into a hopeless nostalgia that is at the root of contemporary supremacism. Supremacism is an expression of older people’s fears. For example, it is because they fear migration that they view it as an invasion.

And, largely, it is an invasion. One or two hundred years ago, racism was an integral part of the invasion by white people of the Southern territories of the world. Nowadays, racism is the fearful reaction by white people to the perceived invasion of their own territories. And the racist paranoia of the great racial “substitution” is not merely a phantom, because it corresponds to a real process (one that is happening without the aid of a conspiracy involving George Soros). The white race is—thank God—disappearing. This is the root of contemporary supremacism, which is simultaneously impotent and hyper-powerful; it is unable to change a future of certain decline, but at the same time, it is perfectly able to destroy the world in desperate acts that aim to reassert a potency that has vanished.

“Impotence” is the word that explains what is happening, particularly in the Northern parts of the planet. Impotence and the desire for revenge. The neoliberal left has destroyed any possible expectation of a political transformation for the future. The neoliberal left: the Clintons, the Blaires, the D’Alemas, François Hollande, and so on. These traitors have destroyed any possibility of expecting something meaningful from politics and from reason. Reason, for its part, has become the servant of financial algorithms. When reason is the financial algorithm, the only thing that we can expect from the future is revenge—indeed, a revenge against reason. Horkheimer and Adorno speak of this revenge against reason in the preface to the *Dialectic of Enlightenment*. They write that if reason is unable to grasp its dark side, the unconscious dark side of reason itself, then reason ensures its damnation. It is dead. Revenge against reason is the driving force of the neo-reactionary movement that is spreading: it is revenge against humanity itself.

Humanity as a cultural horizon has become the main enemy of the contemporary fascists who are not fascists. They are simply antihuman. That would be a kind definition for Matteo Salvini, for a guy who has built his fortune on his declared determination to kill people who come to Europe via the Mediterranean Sea. But remember that Salvini, the right-wing killer, a murderer in the Italian government, is only continuing the political attitudes and applying the rules written by Marco Minniti, the former leftist minister of the interior, who, before Salvini, passed laws that criminalized nongovernmental organizations that rescue people at sea. Salvini is the direct continuation of a democratic murderer named Marco Minniti. Therefore, it is clear that a political way out of this situation does not exist.

WHERE DO WE GO FROM HERE?

I recently read *Staying with the Trouble* by Donna Haraway. When I read Haraway, I don't understand everything, but I glean the essentials. She says, in an ironic and beautiful way, that today there are two reactions to technology. On one side, there are the techno-optimists, who believe that technology will save humanity, the planet, and the environment. On the other side are the techno-apocalyptics, who say, *no way, technology will destroy everything*. Haraway takes a different stance: she instead tells us to keep calm. She says that it isn't a tragedy that the human race is doomed to disappear. Extinction is the new buzzword on the political scene nowadays. Look at the enormous demonstrations organized by children in Sweden, in Germany, in Italy, everywhere in the world. Millions of children marched on March 15, 2019. Their message is about extinction. They don't have a political problem. They simply say: "it's time to panic." And look at Extinction Rebellion. It's the first time in human history, as far as I know, that extinction has become the core concern of a political protest movement. I would not focus on rebelling against extinction. Can one even rebel against extinction? I don't think so. You can *deal* with extinction. You *must* deal with extinction. Extinction, by the way, is not the worst thing that one can imagine for the future. The worst thing imaginable is the war that will lead to extinction—not death, but the long-lasting agony that financial capitalism has prepared for humankind. This is the real danger. Extinction is not so bad, if we compare it to capitalism. After quoting Haraway, I want to quote the French philosopher and psychoanalyst Catherine Malabou. She says that psychoanalysis has undergone a shift from the analysis of sex and language to neurology. The fields of sex and language have long been the focus of psychoanalytic theory and therapy. But when we speak of Alzheimer's and Parkinson's, or of panic attacks and depression, we can see that they're not just problems related to sex and language. They concern the physical dimensions of neurology. It's neurology nowadays that is at stake. It's the brain, not the mind. Or, better yet, it's not *only* the mind, but *also* the brain.

Evolution must be rethought from scratch, from the point of view of the relationship between desire and pleasure. Pleasure is the goal, the aspiration. Over the past forty years, I forgot about pleasure, because I was obsessed with desire, but now I understand that the way out of capitalism is the opposite: the way out is not desire, it is pleasure. And how can the brain find a new balance of pleasure in the present? This is the problem that we are going to face in the coming years, in the coming decade.

I want to dedicate this inconsistent essay to a friend who died in May 2019. The name of this friend is Nanni Balestrini. Nanni was a poet, a novelist, and most of all a recombiner. He is the first poet in history of humankind who never wrote a single word. He refused the dirty work of writing words. He asked: why should I do that? Why should I spend my time writing words? I'm a poet. I don't write words. I take signs from the infosphere, from the daily conversations of people in the subway, from newspapers, from advertisements. His activity, he said, was to recombine. Recombination is also our task, and we should take a cue from him. But the question is: the recombination of what? The recombination of meaning, of language, of desire, of pleasure. Poetry is the consistent and intentional recombination of what exists, with the aim of creating what does not yet exist.

THE AMERICAN ABYSS

2020

FRANCO "BIFO" BERARDI

SURFING THE WAVES OF THE UNKNOWN

During the summer of 2016, I was writing the last chapters of my book titled *Futurability: The Age of Impotence and the Horizon of Possibility*, where I outlined the prospect of a bifurcation. Either social solidarity and conscious subjectivity will be reconstituted, or the world will be drawn into a new form of global fascism. In that context, I was obliged to confront the impending American elections, given that, after Brexit in June of that year, the victory of Donald Trump became possible. Both of these events were symptoms of a widespread psychosis invading the global brain.

That book was not especially about America, nor about elections, nor about Trump. Nevertheless, a consideration of the American scenario was crucial to understanding trends in human evolution.

Now, in summer 2020, Trump seems to be drowning, but it's hard to say what will happen next. The man has many arrows in his quill, even if his victory becomes more unlikely. He is already sending signals of his unwillingness to accept the results of the election; he is already hinting at Democratic Party fraud; and, most dangerously, he has referred his followers several times to the Second Amendment, which, in plain words, is a threat to trigger a wave of armed violence.

I know that it is dangerous to write in simultaneity with events that nobody can precisely foresee, that can only be vaguely intuited. But the only way to imagine something about the becoming of the psycho-sphere is to run ahead of the dynamics of the disaster. My job is not fortune-telling, so I will not engage in predictions about the results of the American elections, but my point is that, whatever happens in November 2020, a conflagration has been sparked in the US that will bring increasing violence, and that this, in due time, will lead to the explosion of the federal state, with unimaginable geopolitical implications.

THE UNMAKING OF THE USA

I would say that the main historical thread of the last twenty years of world history is the not-so-slow disintegration of the US. Of course, the September 11 attacks are one starting point for this unbelievable process. This is by far the most powerful country in the history of the world: the most armed, the most aggressive, the least accessible, protected as it is by two oceans. The only way to destroy it is to turn the giant against itself.

This is exactly what Osama bin Laden's strategy achieved. Under the unintelligent direction of Dick Cheney and George W. Bush, the giant engendered a process of self-destruction. The quagmire of Afghanistan, and then the quagmire of Iraq, provoked a sort of self-destroying fury in the American brain. Salman Rushdie recounted this with some in a book published in 2001 titled *Fury*. Then came the financial collapse of 2008 and the election of a Black president. Barack Obama in the White House was a shock for the supremacist instinct, deeply rooted in American history and in the white American psyche.

The rise of Trump must be viewed as the effect of the white reaction to a long list of perceived humiliations: defeats in two wars, the impoverishment of the middle class in the wake of the 2008 financial crisis, and a sophisticated, elegant Black person dancing in the rooms of the White House. Four years of Trump have almost finalized the disintegration process of the structures of the US state. In 2020, this process was almost complete when the pandemic erupted and swept the country.

What's next? Obviously, I do not know, but I have noticed that, after a series of political setbacks, Trump has turned into the leader of the people of the Second Amendment. When the most recent Black Lives Matter protests spread across the country in June 2020, and earlier, when a group of Trumpists entered the Michigan state capitol building with their weapons drawn, the likely backdrop of the next five years was exposed.

Trump called for the army to crush the riots, and the army said no, defying the word of the president. Then he sent federal troops to Portland, fueling rage and escalating the riots. Is he pointing to a fully-fledged fight just before the elections?

"The Masked Versus the Unmasked" is the title of a May 2020 article published in the *New York Times* by a liberal, moderately progressive, highly educated journalist—actually, my favorite American journalist, Roger Cohen. The title promises something enigmatic, but the text is very clear from the very first lines:

> A neighbor in Colorado would tell me it was time for liberals to "gun up." The other side was armed, he argued, and would stop at nothing. What would we tell our grandchildren when Ivanka Trump took office as the 46th president of the United States in 2025 and term limits were abolished? That we tried words, all manner of them, he scoffed, but they had the rifles.[1]

Unsurprisingly, Cohen immediately adds that he disagrees with his neighbor and that American democracy has nothing in common with Hungarian democracy. I'm not sure that his optimism is well founded.

Even if Viktor Orbán is a fascist and Hungarian democracy is in very bad shape, I'm sorry to say that American democracy is even worse, because it is the expression of the American people, and they are the product of centuries of genocide, of deportations, of slavery, and of systematic violence.

American democracy has been a fake since the beginning, when slave owners who wrote the Declaration of Independence stopped for a moment to consider the possibility of writing something about the problem of slavery, but instead decided to postpone such discussions indefinitely.

We should not conclude that Trump is an aberration of the American spirit, or the exception in a country of sensible people: he is the perfect representation of the white unconscious, pestered by a devastating sense of guilt resulting from the genocide

1. Roger Cohen, "The Masked Versus the Unmasked," *New York Times*, May 15, 2020.

of the native population, the forcible importation of millions of Africans, the long-lasting oppression of Black slaves, military aggression against countless populations, the nuclear annihilation of Hiroshima and Nagasaki, the killing of millions of Vietnamese people, the extermination of Chilean democracy, the killing of Salvador Allende and of thirty thousand people after September 11, 1973. Not to mention the phosphorus bombing of Fallujah and the uncountable victims of the catastrophic wars in Afghanistan and Iraq.

Thanks to his ignorance and moral abjection, Donald Trump represents the true soul of America, the unmovable soul of a population formed by a never-ending sequence of exploitation, oppression, bullying, invasions, and abominable crimes. Nothing but this. There isn't an alternative America, as many thought in the 1960s and '70s. There are millions of women and men, mostly nonwhite, who have suffered from American violence, and who, especially at certain points in the '60s and '70s, fought to reform America to become more human. They failed because there is no way to reform a nation of bigots and killers.

Now more than ever, however, it is possible to envision the opportunity to destroy America, not to reform it. And this is possible because America is destroying itself. Osama bin Laden succeeded in his attempt to turn the greatest military power against itself. The 9/11 provocation succeeded in drawing the giant into a war against chaos. Those who wage war against chaos are doomed, because chaos feeds upon war.

In 1992, when George Bush Sr. said at the first summit on climate change in Rio de Janeiro that the lifestyle of the American people was not subject to negotiation, we learned that the planet faces a dilemma regarding its future: unless America is broken, humankind will not survive.

In the American literary consciousness, we can find countless footprints of this horrible manifest destiny, and in the following paragraphs I want to retrace some of them. At first, I considered writing about the books of Joyce Carol Oates, particularly *American Martyrs* (2017), or of those by Octavia Butler, especially the dystopian premonition of *The Parable of the Sower* (1993). Instead,

I decided to speak only of white males, so that the abyss may be described from the inside: Cormac McCarthy, John Steinbeck, Philip Roth, and Jonathan Franzen. I know that this is a debatable choice, and some may reproach me for it. I am reproaching myself for this choice, but I excuse myself for a very personal reason: I am male, I am white, I am old. I know what I'm talking about.

INNER DARK

Cormac McCarthy's second novel, *Outer Dark*, published in 1968, may be read as a metaphorical journey back to the original soul of white America. The time and the place of the story are nebulous: wilderness, the absence of historical references, and a pervasive sense of obfuscation.

Somewhere in Appalachia, sometime around the turn of the twentieth century, a woman named Rinthy gives birth to her brother's baby. The brother, Culla, leaves the nameless infant in the woods to die, and eventually tells the sister that the baby died of natural causes. The woman does not trust him, and goes away, into the darkness, looking for the child.

"The children of the kingdom shall be cast out into outer darkness: there shall be weeping and gnashing of teeth," reads the Gospel of Matthew. The oppressive presence of the Biblical God is in the background of the book: the shadows of guilt obsessively haunt the characters of the novel, but no consciousness emerges from their actions or from their words.

After abandoning the child, Culla goes wandering and looking for a job (what else?). He finds a job and weapons, kills a squire, then finds a new job, then flees from the police. Nothing makes sense. Culla's actions are like fragmentary memories of a nightmare. The final episode of his journey is the most absurd, and the most creepy: Culla falls into a river, breaks his leg, and comes out from the water to meet three people who have been following him. These three men are carrying his abandoned son. The child is horribly wounded, with an injured eye. The men accuse Culla of fathering the child and of abandoning him. Then one of the trio slays the baby.

The ending of the novel is swathed in the surrealistic light of madness: after surviving his creeping adventures, Culla makes friends with a blind man. He watches the blind man walk towards a swamp, towards certain death. The novel ends with Culla thinking: "Someone should tell a blind man before setting him out that way."

The fake glory of the colonization of the West is recounted here as a nightmare, as a foggy meandering between violence and fear and abjection.

WRATH

From the nightmare of McCarthy to the historical reality of John Steinbeck: I was reminded of the most important American novel of the 1930s while reading an article from the far-right libertarian financial blog *Zero Hedge*, an interesting reference point for white supremacy.

As a reader of this repugnant but useful rag, my attention was captivated one day by an article titled "The Old America Is Dead: Three Scenarios For The Way Forward." Written by Wayne Allenswroth, the article is about John Steinbeck's novel *The Grapes of Wrath* and the 1939 film adaption by John Ford.

The novel stages a community of farmers in Oklahoma in the days of the Great Depression. Due to debt and to the financial context that the farmers are unable to understand, one day they receive a visit from the landowner's men, who bring the message that they are to be evicted:

> Some of the owner men were kind because they hated what they had to do, and some of them were angry because they hated to be cruel ... And all of them were caught in something larger than themselves. Some of them hated the mathematics that drove them, and some were afraid, and some worshiped the mathematics because it provided a refuge from thought and from feeling. If a bank or a finance company owned the land, the owner man said, The Bank—or the Company—needs—wants—insists—must

> have—as though the Bank or the Company were a monster, with thought and feeling, which had ensnared them ... The bank—the monster has to have profits all the time. It can't wait. It'll die.[2]

Here, Steinbeck describes, in a quite vivid way, the impotence that workers and functionaries experience when facing the monster of financial capitalism. But the interesting thing is that the pro-Trump *Zero Hedge* resurrects Steinbeck now, as the scenario of the Depression returns through the conditions triggered by the pandemic. Steinbeck continues:

> At last the owner men came to the point. The tenant system won't work anymore. One man on a tractor can take the place of twelve or fourteen families. Pay him a wage and take all the crop. We have to do it. We don't like to do it. But the monster's sick.[3]

The tenants sit on the ground while the landowner's lawyer finally tells them:

> You'll have to get off the land. The plows'll go through the dooryard.
>
> And now the squatting men stood up angrily. Grampa took up the land, and he had to kill the Indians and drive them away. And Pa was born here, and he killed weeds and snakes. Then a bad year came and he had to borrow a little money. An' was born here. And Pa had to borrow money. The bank owned the land then, but we stayed and we got a little bit of what we raised.[4]

2. John Steinbeck, *The Grapes of Wrath* (Viking, 1939), 32–33.
3. Steinbeck, *Grapes of Wrath*, 34.
4. Steinbeck, *Grapes of Wrath*, 34.

But the owner's men are inflexible:

> We're sorry. It's not us. It's the monster. The bank isn't like a man …
>
> The tenants cried, Grampa killed Indians, Pa killed snakes for the land. Maybe we can kill banks—they are worse than Indians and snakes …
>
> And now the owner men grew angry. You'll have to go.
>
> We'll get our guns, like Grampa when the Indians came. What then?
>
> Well—first the sheriff, and then the troops. You'll be stealing if you try to stay, you'll be murderers if you kill to stay. The monster isn't men, but it can make men do what it wants.[5]

These pages illuminate the sentiment and the mythology that lie beneath Trump and make up his strength. The white people who earned this land by killing Indigenous people are under threat because of liberal globalism. Trump is their weapon against the globalist threat. The people of the Second Amendment are facing their last opportunity to save their social dominance: this opportunity is Trump. Just read what Allensworth writes in *Zero Hedge*:

> Our people, our culture, our history, everything we hold dear, is under relentless attack by the Main Stream Media, politicians, "activists," and kritarchs in the courts, aided and abetted by enemies within, often our own kith and kin, who have internalized the blood-libel Leftist narrative of an irredeemably "racist" America that must be razed to the ground … Our enemy, in this case is the globalist Blob and its militant would-be Che Guevaras and LARPing Leninists, the MSM, the bureaucracy, the courts, the big corporations, and the education establishment. Yet, for the most part, until recently, the Blob has not confronted the Historic American Nation head-on. The Blob has been

5. Steinbeck, *Grapes of Wrath*, 35.

> patient, killing us by the death of a thousand cuts, taking ground steadily through subversion, using propaganda and misinformation, censorship via Tech Totalitarians, and the slow encroachment of what the late Sam Francis called "anarcho-tyranny," with mass immigration ("the Great Replacement") as its weapon of mass destruction. The Blob is amorphous, a slippery, slimy thing that probes and gropes its way into whatever social-economic-political cracks it can exploit, eventually engulfing its prey like quicksand ... Then Donald Trump was elected president. The Blob was shocked. Orange Man Bad seemed to threaten its plans to finish off the Historic American Nation. And so, ever since November 8, 2016, the MSM have kept the country in hysterics with one manufactured crisis after another. Fake news via a social media, a hybrid warfare tactic, kicked into high gear: Russiagate, Ukrainegate, the Chinese Virus panic and ensuing lockdown and economic crash, and now the myth of St. George Floyd and blacks being "hunted" by whites that catalyzed the mobs that have looted and burned American cities. Using the Chinese Virus and Floyd riots as cover, the Blob and its militant wing—Antifa and Black Lives Matter—ratcheted up anarcho-tyranny to new heights.[6]

This narrative is rooted in racialized memory and supported by an army of white people who own weapons and who Trump has unified with the definition "people of the Second Amendment." At the end the article, Allensworth turns to an open invitation to prepare for civil war:

> If we bank solely on electoral politics, we will lose, especially as the demographic ring closes. The winners will show no quarter. Political life as we knew it in America is over. Again, the America we grew up in and loved is dead. Elections

6. Wayne Allenswroth, "The Old America Is Dead: Three Scenarios For The Way Forward," *Zero Hedge*, June 29, 2020.

> are a holding action at best. It seems highly unlikely that Trump (or anyone else, for that matter) can, for instance, deport and encourage to self-deport tens of millions of illegal aliens, even assuming a desire to do so.[7]

The claim is that Trump cannot do the job alone: "we" must take our weapons and do the job: deport tens of millions of illegal aliens, right? We did it a century ago, when we deported Indigenous people, when we slaughtered them. And now, goes the logic of the racist white position, we must do it again.

Madness, yes, but what the political pundits cannot grasp is the following: madness, and only madness, is now ruling a world that is totally out of control.

Allensworth wonders, *What if Trump loses the election in November?* And this is his answer:

> Trump loses, and the Blob and its allies triumph. But because this is a country now and not a nation, with no shared sense of common identity and agreed-upon history, culture, beliefs, or language, only a full-blown police state can hold it together. Even that might not ensure order in a chaotic post-America, and the diminishing number of whites will surely not enjoy the protection of the state. At some point, white Americans might well be living like white South Africans, ever in fear for their lives. If order breaks down, vigilante groups, even criminal gangs, will step into the void, as vigilantes have done in Mexico and Hispanic gangs have done to protect their neighborhoods during the Floyd riots. The good news: white men have followed suit when mobs threatened their homes and history.[8]

7. Allensworth, "Old America is Dead."
8. Allensworth, "Old America is Dead."

THE UNITED STATES IS FRIGHTENING

From the years of the Great Depression, I jump to the 1960s, when progressive consciousness spread out from Black revolts and from university movements.

In *American Pastoral*, Philip Roth stages the tragedy of a man who has grown up in with a somnambulant trust in the American Dream. Suddenly, he is obliged to face the reality of a mental breakdown that traverses his family, his village, his country, and the world. He is called the Swede, but he is a young Jewish man from New Jersey. He's tall, handsome, a good baseball player. We are in the '50s, and life looks joyful and glorious for him. He marries Miss New Jersey, and they have a child, Meredith, a.k.a. Merry. Merry is affected by a pronounced stutter. There's no way to heal this flaw, this small stain on the picture of perfect American joy at the beginning of the '60s.

Then Kennedy is killed, and one day, while Merry is watching TV, she's shocked by the image of a Vietnamese monk, dressed in saffron, who lights himself on fire and stays still until the moment he falls, a human inferno. For Merry, this is the beginning of a monstrous mutation. She recoils from this image, she cries, she babbles. Then more Vietnamese monks kill themselves, and the girl's brain is forever scrambled.

The new American reality tears a whole in the fenced-off garden of the Swede's American Dream. The Black uprisings erupt: Watts is on fire, Newark is on fire. The Swede protects the factory that his father bequeathed to him. But everything is changing all around him. Most importantly, Merry has gone crazy: she does not come back home at night, spending her nights with communists and anarchists instead.

Then comes the tragedy, the irredeemable tragedy. Merry becomes a murderer, a terrorist: she sets off a bomb that kills an innocent passerby. Merry is on the run, Merry will never come back, her mother has a nervous breakdown. Then Merry meets up secretly with her father, but she is as thin as a rake, she's dirty, she's ruined. Merry has been raped.

The world of the Swede has broken down, but he must resist, the factory must go on, his wife is out of her mind, she's fucking the heinous neighbor, an intellectual. The Swede calls his brother, his cynical brother, and tells him that nothing is left of his world. His brother replies:

> "You think you know what this country is? You have no *idea* what this country is ... This country is *frightening*. Of course she was raped. What kind of company do you think she was keeping? Of course out there she was going to get raped ... She enters that world, that loopy world out there, with what's going on out there—what do you *expect*?"[9]

Earlier in the same chapter Roth writes:

> Yes, at the age of forty-six, in 1973, almost three-quarters of the way through the century that with no regard for the niceties of burial had strewn the corpses of mutilated children and their mutilated parents everywhere, the Swede found out that we are all in the power of something demented. It's just a matter of time, honky. We all are![10]

It's just a matter of time, says Roth. We are all under the power of something demented. Now the time has come, I guess.

No one would have ever fathomed that America—the greatest country in the world with "the greatest economy ever"—could be on the cusp of another civil war. Now, after more than one hundred and seventy thousand dead in the unspeakable massacre that the American health system has committed, after the killing of George Floyd and the explosion of protests with continuous escalations in police violence, after Trump's warning about the coming electoral fraud by the Democrats, after the call-to-arms he issued to the people of the Second Amendment, after the lines of people

9. Phillip Roth, *American Pastoral* (Houghton Mifflin, 1997), 276.
10. Roth, *American Pastoral*, 256.

buying weapons in the early days of the pandemic, after the armed mobs protesting against the lockdown, I think that civil war is the most likely prospect for this country that is the terminal malady of humankind.

SENILITY

> The madness of an autumn prairie cold front coming through. You could feel it: something terrible was going to happen. The sun low in the sky, a minor light, a cooling star. Gust after gust of disorder. Trees restless, temperatures falling, the whole northern religion of things coming to an end.[11]

This is the opening of *The Corrections*, Jonathan Franzen's 2001 novel that marks the passage to the new century—a century of swift disintegration, beginning with the disintegration of the human brain:

> Alfred lacked the neurological wherewithal. Alfred's cries of rage on discovering evidence of guerrilla actions—a Nordstrom bag surprised in broad daylight on the basement stairs, nearly precipitating a tumble—were the cries of a government that could no longer govern.[12]

Alfred Lambert is an old father of three and husband to Enid. The Lambert family is the protagonist of the novel.

Indeed, *The Corrections* is an account of the decomposition of the American brain, through the story of a couple of old people: Enid, a woman on the brink of depression who discovers the magic of psycho-pharmaceuticals, and Alfred, who is wandering on the border of Alzheimer's disease.

11. Jonathan Franzen, *The Corrections* (Picador, 2002), 3.
12. Franzen, *The Corrections*, 6–7.

The world is getting less and less comprehensible, objects are sliding out of hands, actions get confused, overlap, lose their meaning and their functional relationships.

Not only because of neuro-chemical degradation, but also because of the transformation of the mental environment, reality has grown incomprehensible for the old brain:

> [B]lack man performing oral sex on white man, camera shooting over left hip sixty degrees bemud full profile, crescent of high values curving over buttock, knuckles of black fingers duskily visible in their probing on the dark side of this moon. She downloaded the image and viewed it at high resolution. She was sixty-five years old and she'd never seen a scene like this. She'd fashioned images all her life and she'd never appreciated their mystery. Now here it was. All this commerce in bits and bytes, these ones and zeros streaming through servers at some midwestern university. So much evident trafficking in so much evident nothing. A population glued to screens and magazines.[13]

Astonishment, sorrow, and absurdity are spreading everywhere.

> And there was a very important question that he still wanted answered. His children were coming, Gary and Denise and maybe even Chip, his intellectual son. It was possible that Chip, if he came, could answer the very important question.
>
> And the question was. The question was: [14]

I use the word "senility" to refer to a condition of extreme dissociation of cerebral flow and the surrounding universe; it happens when the brain loses nervous system integration that is needed to consistently elaborate both semiotic and natural impulses. Senility, thus,

13. Franzen, *The Corrections*, 303.
14. Franzen, *The Corrections*, 159.

is an individual condition that is encapsulated in a confused mental state of the old mind. But the expanding presence of old people spreads this condition well beyond the limit of a marginal pathology. Many signs in the present American situation point to a political diagnosis: the American brain is irreversibly rotten.

But before political senility, it is psychological senility. And before being psychological, it is a neurological dysfunction.

The contemporary widespread perception of an apocalyptic vertigo is not only generated as a reckoning with the long history of racial violence, industrial pollution, and economic hyper-exploitation. It is also the result of widespread neurological degradation, and of the inability of the American mind to come to terms with senility and impotence.

In the movie *Nebraska* (2014), directed by Alexander Payne, a police officer discovers Woody Grant walking on the highway. Woody is then picked up by his son David, who learns that Woody wants to go to Lincoln, Nebraska, to collect a million-dollar sweepstakes prize he believes he has won. When David sees the sweepstakes letter, he knows immediately that it is a mail scam designed to get gullible people to purchase magazine subscriptions. David brings his father home, where his mother Kate becomes increasingly annoyed by Woody's insistence on collecting the money.

It is a heartbreaking story, the story of people (most white Americans) who have grown up with fake mythologies and have been nourished with horrible food (in both the physical and spiritual sense), and who are now sleepwalking towards the swamp but still trust in their superiority.

UN-AMERICAN *QUICHOTTE*

In the surrealistic baroque of the novel *Quichotte*, Salman Rushdie recounts the story of an Indian-born writer living in America, who works for an opioid pharmaceutical enterprise (the producers of Oxycontin, by the way) and falls in love with an Indian-born TV star. He travels from California to New York City with his fictional son Sancho Panza and is confronted by countless acts of racist rejection and aggression from the true white Americans, who do not love the brown pair.

> "I want us to speak to each other in that language, especially in public, to defy the bastards who hate us for possessing another tongue."[15]

This is the best definition of Americans: those bastards who hate us for possessing another tongue (and also, it must be said, for speaking better English than they do).

Ignorance is the bedrock of American supremacy. They know nothing about the world, about the numerous and infinitely different countries of the world, they do not speak any language except an impoverished form of English, they do not know, and they protect their ignorance as the origin of their strength. And they have some reason to do this, because ignorance has been the force of those who don't want to be distracted by beauty, by unpredictability, by complexity, so that they can focus only on winning the miserable game of competition, profit, accumulation.

This has been the force of the American people during the last two centuries. But now?

Don't forget that there is another side of American power, which is the contrary of ignorance: knowledge. American universities and other cultural enterprises are the places where knowledge is stored, processed, transformed, created. By whom? By people who come from India, Japan, Italy, China, and many other countries. Silicon Valley would be nothing without the Syrian Steve Jobs, without the Tamil Indian Sundar Pichai, and countless engineers and designers who come from all over the world. The movie industry would be nothing without Italians and Jews. And so on, and so on.

The ambiguous greatness of America has been the result of the marriage between Anglo-Saxon brutality (and ignorance) and cosmopolitan curiosity.

Now, for the first time in history, the integration of these two cultural components is breaking down. The anti-global reaction

15. Salman Rushdie, *Quichotte* (Random House, 2020), 151.

wants to expel, to forbid, to reject, to build walls, erase multiplicity, and reduce complexity.

The core of the process of disintegration is to be found here: in the social blame surrounding intelligence, irony, consciousness, and imagination.

TOO MUCH AND NOT ENOUGH

Then I read the e-book (not all of it, for God's sake) that Mary Trump has devoted to the psychoanalysis of her uncle. *Too Much and Never Enough: How My Family Created the World's Most Dangerous Man* is a useful book, written with some understanding of the psychoanalytic background of the current catastrophic situation. The author is not only a professional psychologist, but also the niece of this horrible man, whose life has been miserable, as is often the case with people who are obliged to defend a self-image that is profoundly fake.

Trump's father, Fred, was a highly functional sociopath, according to Mary Trump. After describing the philosophy that the father transmitted to his son, Mary comments: "Fred's fundamental beliefs about how the world worked—in life, there can be only one winner and everybody else is a loser (an idea that essentially precluded the ability to share) and kindness is weakness—were clear."[16]

Then Mary recounts some family anecdotes. After having a bowl of mashed potatoes thrown on his head, Donald Trump feels humiliated:

> Everybody laughed, and they couldn't stop laughing. And they were laughing *at* Donald. It was the first time Donald had been humiliated by someone he even then believed to be beneath him. He hadn't understood that humiliation was a weapon that could be wielded by only one person in a fight. That Freddy, of all people, could draw him into a

16. Mary L. Trump, *Too Much and Never Enough: How My Family Created the World's Most Dangerous Man* (Simon & Schuster, 2020), 43.

> world where humiliation could happen to *him* made it so much worse. From then on, he would never allow himself to feel that feeing again. From then on, he would wield the weapon, never be at the sharp end of it.[17]

In Mary's opinion, Donald has a double problem: he had too much and not enough. Too much ego, a resentful ego, nourished by a father incapable of providing affection. And not enough love, because his mother was sick, absent, and psychologically dependent on the sociopath.

This looks like a good introduction to the psychogenesis of the president of the United States of America. But also, I guess, it's a good introduction to the psychogenesis of American white males, and of America itself: the psychogenesis of the American abyss.

17. Trump, *Too Much and Never Enough*, 46.

MORE ON THE AMERICAN ABYSS

2021

Even if it is not very original, an essay published by Timothy Snyder in the *New York Times Magazine* on January 9 has a beautiful title: "The American Abyss." The text, however, is disappointing. Snyder writes:

> Post-truth is pre-fascism, and Trump has been our post-truth president. When we give up on truth, we concede power to those with the wealth and charisma to create spectacle in its place. Without agreement about some basic facts, citizens cannot form the civil society that would allow them to defend themselves. If we lose the institutions that produce facts that are pertinent to us, then we tend to wallow in attractive abstractions and fictions. Post-truth wears away the rule of law and invites a regime of myth.[1]

I obviously agree with this last point; that said, it explains nothing. What should be explained is why a large part of American society "believes" in systematically false statements. By the by: does Snyder think that Trumpists "believe" in the words of Trump in a literal sense?

In the 1983 book *Les Grecs ont-ils cru à leurs mythes?* (Did the Greeks believe in their myths?), Paul Veyne questions the meaning of "belief." His conclusion is that the force of mythology does not consist in believing a metaphor literally, in forgetting about the brackets before and after the metaphoric enunciation. Mythological belief (like memetic contagion) today similarly enables a sort of pragmatic coherence in the life of "believers." It gives sense to the world of those who heed such mythology, amidst a world that has lost any sense.

For example, believing Trump's assertion "I won the election" is not a semiological mistake. Rather, it is a strategy for identitarian self-assertion. When liberals speak of "fake news," they totally miss the point, because those who share a mythology (or a meme)

1. Timothy Snyder, "The American Abyss," *New York Times Magazine*, January 9, 2021. I published an essay with the same title in the September 2020 issue of *e-flux journal*.

are not searching for the factual truth, like a social scientist might. Instead, they are consciously or unconsciously using the force of the fake enunciation as an exorcism, as an insult, as a weapon.

The more important question to ask is not why Trump lies, but rather why so many people vote for him in the first place. What are the conditions—economic, political, semiological, and so on—that produce this voting and acting? The solution to the problem is not to impeach the orange man (again), or to ban him from Twitter (too late, Mr. Dorsey, too late). Rather, it is to allow people to think and to choose in a way that is not clouded by humiliation and resentment.

The American crisis is not generated by the perverted effects of mass communication. It is generated by the contradictions that emerge from the racist nature of the most violent country of all time.

The American lifestyle can be summarized in one statistic: the average American consumes four times as much electricity as the average non-American. White Americans—some of whom were impoverished by the 2008 financial crash, from which only the finance class emerged victorious; who feel humiliated by 50 years of criminal wars ignominiously lost; who worry about the coming loss of demographic dominance—are desperately clinging to what little they still have: their SUVs, their weapons, and the right to eat enormous amounts of animals. Endangered by globalization, their privilege is rapidly fading, so they are ready to follow a führer who promises to make America great again.

What happened on January 6 in Washington D.C. was not an insurrection nor a true coup d'état. It was an episode, simultaneously farcical and criminal, in the American civil war between white nationalism and liberal globalism. Both the globalists and the nationalists are expressions of American capitalist supremacy. This civil war is going to endure and expand, and—luckily for humankind—it will consume American potency. If you want to understand the ongoing civil war, you should read an article by American journalist Thomas Frank, published in *Le Monde Diplomatique*, where he points to "new symptoms of [political] degeneration" as reported in a different newspaper:

> Two items from the *Kansas City Star* for 14 July 2020: At a barbecue restaurant near my family's house, a man reportedly walked in wearing a bright red Trump hat but no antiviral face mask. When the kid at the cash register (the kid is paid $8.50 per hour, the paper notes) asked the man to cover his nose and mouth as per local rules, the man flipped up his shirt like Clint Eastwood in an Italian western to let the kid see that he was carrying a pistol.[2]

This exemplifies the prevalence of a creeping civil war in the fabric of everyday American life, which will continue to periodically explode like it did on January 6. This low-intensity war is going to become the norm, and, little by little, it will drag the police and the military into the fray.

The abyss is not semiological, but cultural, social, and racial. White supremacy is the central foundation of American identity because the United States is based on genocide and slavery. Trump is not a malignant exception, but the authentic soul of white America. *This* is the abyss, not the spread of ridiculous lies that only white liberals take seriously.

The Thirteenth Amendment did not abolish slavery in the US. It merely legalized it, so that cotton fields have been replaced by mass incarceration. This is the abyss that Timothy Snyder fails to see.

2. Thomas Frank, "America, the Panic Room," *Le Monde Diplomatique*, October 2020.

COSMISM AND EXTINCTION

2021

The poetics of the artist Anton Vidokle's movies belongs to the imagination of extinction. Paradoxically, we can understand his poetics as both an exorcism and as a pharmacy, as poison and antidote. "Immortality for all," the core of Vidokle's agenda, is the flip side of the otherwise widely felt intuition that the history of human civilization (of humanity itself, perhaps) is potentially drawing to a close. Vidokle translates this contemporary despair into a utopian imagination that calls for universal resurrection, immortality, and access to distant areas of the universe. This is a techno-biological utopia that somewhat paradoxically resonates with the present dystopian zeitgeist.

The primary reference for Vidokle's poetics is Cosmism, a philosophical movement that emerged and thrived at the turn from the twentieth century, in pre- and post-revolutionary Russia, a cultural landscape that was radically different from that of the present. The horizon of that time was marked by expansion as well as technical and social progress. This theoretical and artistic return to Cosmism today comes from the awareness that human civilization is approaching the horizon of extinction. Facing extinction from the point of view of immortality is a way to reactivate all the energies of imagination, of creation, and of struggle in the interest of reversing the contemporary context.

At times, Vidokle's utopia is at odds with my own disposition, which calls for coming to terms with extinction, becoming friends with death, quietly flowing into nothingness. Consciousness has this absolute power: the power to switch out the world. Death is the triumph of consciousness, the annihilation of reality itself—of the universe, planets, earth, history, everything. But this triumph of consciousness is treacherous, because (I know, I know) the surrounding universe does not disappear. It disappears for me, for my sensibility, and for my consciousness, but other subjects go on perceiving, and seeing, and hearing, and enjoying, and suffering.

Thus, Vidokle's vision is different from mine, maybe even the opposite. He envisions a collective participation in self-perception and in the perception of the world, and he defines existence in terms of energy: energy's concretion, energy's combination and recombination. In his movie *This Is Cosmos*, he proclaims: "trees fall ... stars explode / but the number remains the same / always." To understand the meaning of Cosmist delirium, one must start from this declaration: that the relation between energy, matter, and existence is in continuous recombination. Cosmism is a project for comprehending and acting on this recombination as a conscious, political act. Nikolai Fedorovich Fedorov, the original source for the Cosmist movement and the main philosophical reference for Vidokle, demands a new body to host consciousness. He writes: "Philosophy must become the knowledge not only of what is but of what ought to be, that is, from the passive, speculative explanation of existence it must become an active project of what must be, the project of action."[1]

Vidokle is the heir of the Cosmist imagination that runs through the art production from the years of revolution in Russia, coming down from Federov and infiltrating the Futurist enthusiasm of Mayakovsky. The cult of technology and the delusion of technological omnipotence paves the way for the ecstasies of a sort of cosmic communism that sees the resurrection of all as the common task of humanity, to be achievable once emancipated from the petty goals of accumulation.

And so, in addition to its clear connection with mortality and death, capitalism clearly has something to do with immortality, though not for all—it is an immortality predicated on ersatz life through abstract, monetary value. This abstraction, the deceiving lure of infinite growth, the accumulation of value, is the modern way of overcoming human finitude. Furthermore, another identification of immortality with the contemporary lure of mathematical and financial abstraction is also a soulless promise that is doomed to crumble in the end. In fact, it is crumbling, already, in our time, and we are witnessing the slow-motion dismantling of the established order of the economy.

We have witnessed the crumbling of monetary abstraction over the course of our lives, and now I have the feeling that money is going to lose all its charm as well, as death takes the upper hand in

1. Nikolai Fyodorovic Federov, *Filosofiia obshchego dela*, cited in V. V. Zenkovsky, *Istoriia russkoi filosofii*, vol. 2 (IMKA-PRESS, 1950), 135.

the social, psychic, and geopolitical landscapes. Capitalist immortality was based on the imperishability of abstraction. But the Covid-19 pandemic marks the comeback of bodily materiality in the shape of sickness, contagion, and decomposition. Meanwhile, as already mentioned, extinction looms as the horizon of the century.

In the first decades of the past century, Italian and Russian Futurism was represented by a young generation of artists full of energetic expectations: expansion, mechanization, technology, acceleration. No more so today: the new generation of futurists around us is frail and precarious, and the overall population of the Northern Hemisphere is growing old. The West is senescent and frail, while past dreams of glory are giving way to resentment and fear. In the last century, white futurism was all about conquest, expansion, colonization. The contemporary white (supremacist) imagination is instead obsessed with the fear of invasion, of ethnic replacement, and similarly frustrating obsessions. Instead of conquering, they cling to what little they have left. Today, Bezos flies into outer space to escape the burning planet he is helping set ablaze.

In the work of poet and playwright Velimir Khlebnikov (who named himself King of Time and President of the Planet Earth), this transhistorical dimension emerges with the project of a transcognitive language, joining together the potencies of European and Asian mythological backgrounds. Asia and Europe don't just meet in the historical dimension of war and revolution, but in the protohistorical dimension of the origins of language: this is the precondition for the linguistic experiments of Zaum. In Vladimir Mayakovsky's work, the transhistorical dimension emerges with the dreams of extraplanetary travel and of trans-individual survival. In *About That* (*Про это*, 1923), Mayakovsky speaks with a chemist in a distant future and asks for help in resuscitating himself. And Bogdanov, the biologist and Bolshevik theoretician who rivalled Lenin in the philosophical interpretation of historical materialism, also experimented with techniques for rejuvenation and nurtured projects for fostering a culture of immortality.

The nineteenth-century Symbolists, who were more or less coeval to Federov, were extremely conscious of this proximity of poetry and breath, which is not only metaphorical, but deeply inscribed in the psycho-physical rhythm of breathing. Baudelaire spoke of *corrispondence*, referring to this relation between poetic forms and the rhythm of the cosmos. Mallarmé, too, conceived of the poetic word as a rhythmic transformer, as a key to the innermost tempo of the universe. Russian Symbolism emphasized this correspondence up to the point of mystical spiritualism, and, in some cases (like in the case of Klebnikov and Alexsei Kruchyonykh), this correspondence was grounded in scientific (or pseudo-scientific) imagination. Therefore, Cosmism was not an isolated blend of positivist faith in science and mystical imagination. It was the most extreme and visionary expression of a wide movement of techno-mystical utopianism that melted with the political euphoria of the revolution.

In the end, I would say that Vidokle's magnificent obsession is recombinant immortality. This is perfectly opposite, and complementary, to my own obsession: becoming nothing. For me, the triumph of consciousness is the obliteration of the world: we call it death, but we might see it as an act of cosmic potency of the self.

Consciousness is my focus; Vidokle's is energy. We are both crazily wrong, because one obsession cannot exist without the other. I say that consciousness is the condition of the world, and death is the triumph of consciousness, the annihilation of the world. Vidokle says that matter is eternal and that life is limited only because an error occurred: death. He is right, and I am wrong. He is wrong, and I am right. Together, we might glimpse something of the ineffable nature of time.

DESIRE, ENERGY, EXHAUSTION IN THE POST-PANDEMIC LANDSCAPE

2021

DECLINE AND THE EXHAUSTION OF PSYCHOLOGICAL ENERGY

According to what Deleuze and Guattari write in *Anti-Oedipus*, desire is the tension that pushes and drags one towards an object that does not exist, but that is created precisely through the process of reaching out. Far from being the satisfaction of a need, or the filling of a lack, desire is the creation of the other as attractor and projection. The object of desire attracts the subject while also projecting the subject.

Indeed, it is in the sphere of desire that the animating forces of the social sphere are born. Since desire is the strongest attraction, the foundation of the most radical complicity, it drives processes of historical subjectivation. But the explosion and externalization of the unconscious that were provoked by the media-machine in the era of global connection produced a nervous breakdown of energy and triggered a pathological panic–depression cycle. Semiocapitalism is ceaselessly spreading desire, but it is postponing pleasure, because attention-time must be invested in production, consumption, and competition.

The effects of global neoliberal planning have resulted in the exasperation of the fanaticism of limitlessness (growth) that chiefly belongs to Western culture. In the twentieth century, the fanaticism for "no-limits" growth fueled ideology like Marinetti's Futurism that exalted aggressiveness, violence, and war. In the twenty-first century, on the other hand, futurist ideology has been revived by Californian biotechnological transhumanism, a sort of futurism of a senescent hyper-techno society that has lost vital energy and aims to replace it with bio-electronic devices.

Then came the collapse: the Covid-19 pandemic produced a sudden, dramatic slowing of social and psychic rhythms. I would call it psycho-deflation: the deflation of desire, the sanitary interdiction of pleasure. What might reactivate desire so that human evolution can escape the double spiral of chaos and automation, of war and techno-totalitarianism? Is a re-activation of psychological energy even possible? Should we expect that Western culture will be able to deal with its own exhaustion (linked with the limits to economic growth), or should we expect that the white race will react to its own decline with a suicidal aggression unleashed on all of humanity, as has already begun?

A PSYCHO-SOCIAL MUTATION IS UNDERWAY

During the Covid pandemic, the world entered a psycho-social mutation. The long process of oscillation between desire and anxiety, resulting from decades of neoliberal reform and digital connectivity, morphed into a different psycho-landscape that requires deciphering. On the one hand, we notice that, after the pandemic, an aggressive geopolitical landscape has emerged: war at the Eastern border of Europe, rumors of war everywhere else. But, on the other hand, we detect the signs of a sort of psycho-deflation, a resignation of sorts, an abandonment of any faith in the values that mobilized society in past decades.

The imperative of the social superego gives signs of changing direction. In the Freudian view, the superego requires a renunciation of the impulse (*Trieb*) and the pleasure that comes from the immediate satisfaction of desire. On the contrary, the neoliberal imperative is aimed at arousing and mobilizing collective desire (for consumption, generally). It invites the pursuit of a joy that continually escaped, that was unreachable, while stimulating competitive frenzy and frustration.

Now, the superego that emerged during the pandemic is instead founded on caution. It is very likely that this cautious condition (in which erotic emotions become dangerous and problematic) may lead to the furthering of the existing epidemic of depression and may furthermore contribute to the accumulation of a dangerous, aggressive mental energy.

SEXUALITY AND CULTURAL MUTATION

In the 1920s, the psychoanalyst Wilhelm Reich explained the mass psychology of fascism and war as effects of sexual repression imposed by dominant morality and the monogamous family. This explanation was useful for understanding much of the psycho-political dynamics in the age of industrial capitalism, but it lost much of its relevance when, after the 1960s, mass culture was hit by successive waves of sexual liberalization, and then by media and advertising hyper-stimulation that capitalized on the former.

Let's think back to the effects that the AIDS crisis produced in the sexually transgressive landscape of the 1980s, for example. From an aesthetic and cultural point of view, AIDS inaugurated the transition to the anthropology of virtual connection: connectivity separates desire from pleasure, establishes a cycle of excitement that does not reach the pleasure of physical conjunction. Yet that syndrome concerned only a marginal part of the social and erotic landscapes: only the exchange of blood, semen, vaginal fluid, anal mucus, and breast milk could transmit the infection. With Covid, it's different: the exchange of saliva, bodily proximity, even exposure to the breath of someone else can have pathogenic effects.

At the same time, the phobic sensitization to the lips and skin of the other is a danger that goes beyond the direct consequences of the pandemic. There is a danger of mass de-eroticization, which consequently risks inhibiting the most elementary act of relaxation of psychic tension, the act that more than any other mitigates the pain of existing. The pandemic did not produce a complete innovation in this respect, as signs of a syndrome of bodily isolation were already inscribed in the techno-social lifestyle of the first decades of the century, but it represented a precipitation of trends that were already underway in the globalizing and connective transformation. Existing trends have been accelerated by Covid and are now, perhaps, moving toward a real leap in quality, a new evolution of the psychosphere.

EVOLVING DEPRESSION

The meaning of depression is not so clear. First of all, it is not evident to the depressed person, who is generally unable to ascertain exactly why they are depressed. But it's not clear to the psychiatrist who is diagnosing depression either. The philosopher might say that depression is a condition of dangerous proximity to ultimate truth, the one that should not be seen, like the face of Medusa that paralyses the watcher. For our purposes, let us provisionally define depression as a paralysis of the imagination of the future, and as a paralysis of desire, which results in a weakening, or even a nullification of the tension toward reality.

What we do know is that, in the last few decades, diagnoses have skyrocketed to the point that depression is considered the most common pathology among young populations. In the past, other pathologies competed for primacy: in the bourgeois era, when Freud conceptualized the discomfort of civilization and founded a discipline destined to understand the dynamics of the unconscious, neurosis enjoyed (so to speak) first place. The repression of sexual desire, the moral and social obligations that forbade free sexuality, produced neurotic reactions in subjects who were unable to compensate for the frustration of the libido with so-called superior activities aimed at the sublimation of repressed psychic energy.

Then the environment changed, when the repression of libido was replaced by the unleashing of desiring energies, by social and erotic competition, and by the constant acceleration of the psycho-stimulatory machine of global media. At that point, psychotic tendencies took the central place in the attention of psychiatrists. A schizophrenic existential style was promoted by advertising and the neoliberal ideology: "just do it".

Economic profit was recognized as the only value worth considering, up to the point that crime is legitimized if is pursued with the aim of increasing economic growth. The psychotic acceleration of info-neuro stimulation unleashed schizoid-type processes and caused a sort of explosion of the unconscious, externalized in the phantasmagoria of the commodity and its image.

The third decade of the twenty-first century opens with a collapse of hyperstimulated energy by schizo-pathogenic neoliberalism: psycho-deflation, first spread as a consequence of a virus, then ended up settling at the heart of the hyperstimulated organism of society. In September 2020, Canda's chief public health official, Dr. Theresa Tam, suggested skipping kissing and wearing a mask during sexual intercourse. However, going solo, she remarked, remained the safest option.

It is not my intention to discuss the appropriateness of this type of medical advice, which may even have been necessary for reducing the lethal spread of the virus. However, I believe that we should reflect on the psychological, social, and anthropological implications of such a situation, after years of development in this direction. Social distancing was already a developing trend in social life since the Internet turned into a sort of networked replacement for face-to-face communication. The pandemic accelerated this and turned social distancing into an obligation, a lifestyle transforming education, work, and every kind of social interaction.

In the existential experience that we all lived during the pandemic, and particularly in the affective experience of the generation that was born at the turn of the millennium, the contagion caused a trauma, destined to act not only on present behaviors, but also to reshape sensitivity and the unconscious sphere itself. As trauma can affect empathy and particularly erotic sensitivity, we cannot predict what kind of adaptive change is destined to follow.

DEPRESSION AS KNOWLEDGE

Today, interpreting depression is our main political task. Firstly, we must remember that depression is not only, and not even primarily, a pathology. It is also a form of knowledge. Indeed, James Hillman said that depression is the form of knowledge closest to the truth: the truth of the irreversibility of time, the truth of being on the horizon of death. If we consider depression as a form of knowledge, then we can process it from the inside in such a way that it does not produce suffering, but awareness, and, starting from this recognition of the cognitive value of depression, we can free depression from isolation, we can reactivate the imagination.

It is the ambiguity of psycho-deflation that interests me, because this ambiguity can evolve in the sense of desertion: desertion from war, desertion from nationalism, but also from the collective race toward the accumulation of capital – that is, toward the abyss. Interpreting depression is a philosophical, psychoanalytic, and political task.

In 1998, Alain Ehrenberg published *Weariness of the Self: Diagnosing the History of Depression in the Contemporary Age*, in which he captures the essential core of that pathology, or rather of that form of suffering that was spreading in the years of the neoliberal revolution, a depression intimately linked to competition and a sense of failure, of inadequacy.

"The depressed individual is unable to measure up; he is tired of having to become himself," he writes.[1] Then, later, "The business environment is the antechamber of the nervous breakdown."[2] Lastly, concluding on the mobilization of depression in neoliberal workplace culture, he remarks that: "But nowadays the engineers of human relations are working to produce autonomy. They are not trying to make the body submissive; they are hoping to mobilize the affect and mental capacities of each employee."[3]

The neoliberal decades have subjected nervous energies to constant stress and have produced effects of psychic fatigue that have taken the clinical form of depression. Perhaps today we must develop that kind of interpretation to read depression in a different way, no longer as a failure of libidinal investments, but as conscious disinvestment from capital. As resignation.

The present wave of depression is probably a sign of an emerging consciousness of exhaustion. Physical resources of the planet and nervous resources of mind are undergoing a process of exhaustion that cannot be acknowledged by the dominant culture of

1. Alain Ehrenberg, *Weariness of the Self: Diagnosing the History of Depression in the Contemporary Age* (Montreal: McGill-Queen's University Press, 2009), 4.
2. Ehrenberg, 184.
3. Ehrenberg, 184.

competition, productivity, and accumulation. This inability has a psychopathogenic effect on the social mind: as long as we are unable to reframe our social and individual existence in the horizon of exhaustion, we will be exposed to storms of murderous suicidal dementia.

HYPERWORLD, METAWORLD, AND THE END OF THE WORLD

2022

THE HYPERWORLD

All that we needed to know about cyberspace was already written by John Perry Barlow in 1996 in "A Declaration of Independence of Cyberspace":

> On behalf of the future, I ask you of the past to leave us alone. You are not welcome among us. You have no sovereignty where we gather. We have no elected government, nor are we likely to have one, so I address you with no greater authority than that with which liberty itself always speaks. I declare the global social space we are building to be naturally independent of the tyrannies you seek to impose on us. You have no moral right to rule us nor do you possess any methods of enforcement we have true reason to fear.[1]

In thirty years, cyberspace has emerged: a hyperworld which the earthly world can no longer control. The contribution that industrial companies have paid in the form of taxes does not apply to companies that have established a non-territorial sphere. The political powers are not sovereign in the sphere of non-territory; on the contrary, the virtual non-territory has become the global infrastructure without which political, administrative, and economic systems cannot function. The hyperworld is a dimension that recodes social reality by transferring linguistic practices (economy, politics, communication, affectivity) to an accelerated level that is independent of territorial laws. The metaworld is a dimension that not only recodes the world, but also recodes psychic and linguistic subjectivity by translating them for a metaworld of simulated stimuli and perceptions.

In late October 2021, Mark Zuckerberg hosted a conference on a virtual reality platform. This was certainly not in response to

1. John Perry Barlow, "A Declaration of the Independence of Cyberspace," February 8, 1996, available at *Electronic Frontier Foundation*, eff.org.

whistleblower allegations denouncing the harmful effects of social networks—a trivial point in reality, because the exposure of the human mind to an increasing amount of virtual neurostimulation leads to a mutation that goes beyond the political will of censors and moralizers. Those complaints are inconsistent. It is true that Facebook, like other social networks, tends to amplify and radicalize social hatred. But it is not Facebook that has spawned frustration, impotent anger, and hatred. It is the increasingly unequal, precarious, and violent economic system that is the breeding ground for collective aggression. Of course, Facebook is also part of this system. The social networks, from which the warmth of bodies has disappeared, only reinforce this violence while glorifying its ineffectiveness. The more our anger grows, the more pronounced our powerlessness becomes.

THE METAWORLD

The cycle of impotence has probably now reached its ultimate limit, and Zuckerberg is proposing another leap: into the meta-space, for which cyberspace has created the infrastructure. Some critics have noted that Zuckerberg wants to make his system independent of Apple and Google, on which it is currently technically dependent for some functions. In the *New York Times*, Kara Swisher argues that Meta is just a broader corporate structure created by Zuckerberg to escape recent legal troubles.[2] Really? Certainly, Zuckerberg's decisions are in part driven by economic and technical considerations. But the philosophical implications of Meta's launch are much more important in my opinion. The innovation aims to leverage experiments conducted since the 1980s, when Jaron Lanier was the first to talk about virtual reality and synesthetic communication without symbols. Visual and multisensory software has been perfected since then, and now the meta-project is to bring those technologies together into an immersive experience via a platform like Oculus or

2. Kara Swisher, "Escaping Into the Metaverse," *New York Times*, October 29, 2021.

other more advanced transducers of electronic impulses. In his talk, Zuckerberg announced the expansion of the immersive dimension with augmented reality hardware and custom sensors. If Hyper is a dimension that infinitely accelerates the cycle of impulse communication, then Meta is the dimension in which impulse communication simulates and replaces the real relationship between the brain and the world to establish a meta-reality in which the other no longer exists except as simulated nerve stimulation.

The announcement of a leap from Hyper to Meta came in the same days that preparations were being made for the COP26 conference in Glasgow. No realistic plan can reconcile economic growth and the necessary reduction of emissions. So, given the absolute priority of economic growth, promises are being made again: everything will be fine in 2050 (or maybe 2060 or 2070); by then, there will be no one left to verify it. And so, now that we know the world will become uninhabitable, we start building the metaworld. A population of *hikikomori* (Japanese for severe social withdrawal), who will connect from their workplace to a world of perceptual stimuli. Imagination will have finally taken over while the physical and social body rots.

SILENCE

Will the Metaworld work? Will a significant part of the human population move to the simulated sphere? I don't know. What I do know is that one day in October 2021, the entire Facebook system went down for six hours. No one explained what happened, neither Zuckerberg nor anyone else. So let us speculate. The first hypothesis is that it was internal sabotage: Facebook employees expressed themselves in this way for political reasons. Too good to be true, and I think they would have told us. The second hypothesis is that the sabotage was organized from outside—by the usual suspects, Russians or Macedonians or the Chinese, who knows. Possibly, but I don't think that was the case. The third hypothesis is that Zuckerberg, tired of being attacked by the media and the American political system, made a small demonstration: try to see what happens when I block a territory that includes three and a half billion citizens, countless companies that produce, distribute, advertise, and so on. Possible, realistic even. However, the most likely hypothesis is the simplest: the month the world discovered the first global congestion crisis, or rather hypercomplexity, Facebook also failed, for the simple reason that, somewhere in the infrastructure, there was not enough power, or that the demand for connections at that moment exceeded its limits.

The more complex an integrated system is, the harder it is to locate, isolate, and fix glitches. In the months and years to come, when the world becomes too ugly to bear, we will probably switch to the metaworld. The headphones in our ears will prevent us from hearing the sound of suffering, and the glasses will prevent us from seeing the misery, sadness, and devastation all around us. But at some point, an overload, or perhaps Russian sabotage, or an unpredictable, inexplicable power collapse, will shut down the earphones and all other connecting devices—just as Don DeLillo imagines in his short novel *Silence*. A silence of the grave.

WAR AND SENILE DEMENTIA

2022

ANNIHILATE

Anéantir (Annihilate), the most recent book by Michel Houellebecq, is seven hundred pages long—half that length would have been enough.[1] It isn't the best of his books, but it does succeed in sketching a simultaneously submissive and irate representation of the decline of world domination by the white race.

Somewhere deep in France, a family gathers around their eighty-year-old father, who has suffered a stroke. The patriarch, who had worked for the secret service, has now fallen into an interminable coma. Meanwhile, his son Paul, who also works for the secret service as well as the Ministry of Finance, discovers he has terminal cancer. Aurélien, Paul's brother, kills himself, incapable of continuing a life in which he has always been considered a loser. Lastly, there is the daughter, Cécile, a Catholic fundamentalist. Cécile is married to a fascist notary who lost his job but has found another in the right-wing circle of the Lepenists, still on the rise.

The central theme of this novel is terminal illness. In other words, it is about the agony of Western civilization. It is not a pretty sight, because the white mind does not resign itself to the inescapable. Tragic are the reactions of agonizing, old, white men.

Here, this scene unfolds in contemporary France—a place that has been culturally devasted over the last forty years of neoliberal development. It is a ghost of a country in which political struggle now takes place in the corrupt stages of ultranationalism, racism, Islamophobia, and economic fundamentalism. But this scene does not only unfold in France; it is the condition of the post-global world that is now threatened by the senile delirium of the dominant culture as it falls—that of the white, Christian, imperialist empire.

1. Michel Houellebecq, *Anéantir* (Éditions Flammarion, 2022).

WAR, AGONY, SUICIDE

At the Eastern borders of Europe, two old white men play a game in which neither of them can retreat.

The old white American is on the heels of a humiliating and tragic defeat. Worse than Saigon, Kabul is fresh in the global imaginary as a sign of the cognitive breakdown of the long-dominant, imperialist power. The old white Russian knows that the base of his power is a nationalist promise: to avenge the honor of "Holy Mother Russia." The one who retreats first will lose everything.

The fact that Putin is a Nazi was already clear at the conclusion of the second war in Chechnya. But, at the time, he was still lauded by the American president, who looked him in the eyes and praised his sincerity. The Russian also enjoyed the favor of British banks, as they were filled to the brim with rubles robbed by Putin and his friends through the dismantling of public infrastructures after the fall of the Soviet Union. Geriatric Russians and Anglo-Americans were brothers in arms when it came to destroying the social spheres produced by past labor and communist movements all over the world.

But friendship and camaraderie don't last among assassins. In fact, what use would NATO be if peace was actually brokered? And how would a successful peace have affected the bottom lines of the multinational companies producing weapons of mass destruction and death—today making endless profits? The expansion of NATO only serves to reignite a hostility that capitalism could not let die, to keep the profitable conflict alive.

There is no rational explanation for the war in Ukraine, especially because it is the climactic movement in a psychotic crisis of the white brain. What rationality is there in the expansion of NATO, which arms Polish, Baltic, and, yes, Ukrainian Nazis against Russian Nazism? In exchange, Biden gets the result most feared by American war strategists: forcing Russia and China into an embrace that, fifty years ago, Nixon succeeded in weakening.

Given that the war is inexplicable in strategic terms, to understand the war we don't need to think geopolitically, but rather psycho-pathologically. Perhaps we need a geopolitics of psychotic outbursts. At stake here is the political, economic, demographic, and, finally, psychic defeat of white, Western, (post)colonial civilization, which cannot accept the prospect of exhaustion, which prefers destruction or suicide to the slow extinction of white dominance.

WEST, FUTURE, DECLINE

With the war in Ukraine, a hysterical arms race begins, borders are consolidated (along racialized lines), and violence increases exponentially—all demonstrations of the senile marasmus into which the West has fallen.

On February 23, 2022, when Russian troops were already in the Donbass, Trump praised Putin as a peacekeeping "genius,"[2] and suggested that the US follow his lead on the Mexican border. Let's see if we can figure out what Trump's obscenities mean. Is there a kernel of truth in his delusions? At issue is the very concept of the West. But first, what is the West?

If by "West" we refer to a geographical definition, then Russia is of course excluded. But if we think about the anthropological and historical meanings of that word, then Russia is more Western than any other West. In other words, the West can be defined as the land of decline and of obsession with the future. Those two traits are in fact one, given that, for organisms subject to the second law of thermodynamics—as are individual and social bodies—the future can only mean eventual decline.

We—both the "we" of the West and the Westerners of the boundless Russian lands—are therefore united in futurism and decline, that is, in the delirium of omnipotence and in the desperation of impotence.

Trump gets credit for telling it like it is, claiming that our enemies are not Russians, but migrants from the Global South; China, which we have humiliated; Africa, which we have plundered. Those

2. See Oliver Milman, "Trump Praises 'Genius' Putin for Moving Troops to Eastern Ukraine," *The Guardian*, February 22, 2022.

are our enemies, not the very white Russia, which is part of the "Great West." This Trumpist logic is based on a white supremacy that sees Russianness as the most extreme form of acceptable whiteness.

Biden's logic is instead based on the defense of the "free world": a world born from genocide, from the forced deportation of millions of slaves, and organized around foundational systemic racism. Biden chooses to break the "Great West" apart in favor of a smaller West without Russia, which is in any case destined to tear itself apart and to involve the whole planet in its suicide.

So, let's define the West as a sphere of racist dominance obsessed with the future. Time stretches out in an expansive pulse: economic growth, accumulation, capitalism. It is exactly this obsession with the future that feeds the machine of dominance: a concrete present (of pleasure, of muscular relaxation) is invested into and exchanged for abstract future value.

Perhaps we could reformulate the classical Marxist analysis of value to say that exchange value is precisely this accumulation of the present (the concrete) in abstract forms (like money) that can be exchanged for something else tomorrow.

The fixation on and fetishization of the future are by no means a natural cognitive modality of the human. Most human cultures have been organized around a cyclical understanding of time, or on the insuperable dilation of the present. Futurism is a transition to complete self-consciousness (also in aesthetic terms) of cultures of expansion. But there are many futurisms.

The obsession with the future has different implications in the theological-utopian sphere that is central to Russian culture and the techno-economic sphere of Euro-American culture. Nikolai Federov's cosmism and Vladimir Mayakovsky's futurisms both share an eschatological breath that is lacked by the technocratic fanaticisms of Marinetti and Musk. Maybe that is why it is Russia's destiny to end history—and here we are.

NAZISM IS EVERYWHERE

The new horizon is war that pits one Nazism against another. In his writings from the 1960s, Gunter Anders predicted that the nihilistic charge of Nazism would not die with the defeat of Hitler.[3] He presaged that it would return onto the world stage when technical power developed to such a degree that it provoked the humiliation of the human.

Nazism is reemerging as a psycho-political form of the demented body of the white race, which ragefully reacts to its own unstoppable decline. Viral chaos has created the conditions for the formation of a global, biopolitical infrastructure, but it has also accentuated the widely experienced perception of matter's ungovernability as it loses order, disintegrates, and dies. The West has forsaken death because that concept is not compatible with its obsession with the future. It has rejected senility because it is not compatible with expansion and growth. But now, the (demographic, cultural, and economic) aging of the dominant cultures of the Global North are presented as a specter that white culture cannot even contemplate, let alone accept.

This is where the white brain (that common to Biden and Putin) enters a furious crisis of senile dementia. Then the white brain most lost to senility—that of Donald Trump—utters a truth that no one can stand to hear: Putin is our best friend. Sure, he's a racist murderer, but we are no less so. On the other hand, Biden represents the impotent anger that old people express and feel when they notice the decline of their strength, psychic energy, and cognitive efficiency. Now that exhaustion is in its advanced stage, extinction is the only reassuring prospect.

Can humanity save itself from the murderous violence of the demented and agonized Western, Russian, and European brains?

The invasion of Ukraine will continue, whether it becomes a stable occupation (unlikely) or concludes with the withdrawal

3. See Günther Anders, *The Obsolescence of Humankind* (1956–80), from which only select essays have been translated into English.

of Russian troops after the destruction of the military apparatus donated to Kyiv by the West (more likely). Regardless, the conflict will not be resolved by the defeat of either of two patriarchs. Neither one can accept retreat. Therefore, this invasion signals the beginning of a phase of continuous war that will be global (and that may express itself in nuclear terms). The final war against humanity has begun.

The only thing we can do is to desert, to abandon, to transform fear into thought, to resign ourselves to the inevitable and make way to the unpredictable: peace, pleasure, life.

THE SERPENT'S EGG

2022

BETWEEN DEPRESSION AND AGGRESSIVENESS: THE BIRTH OF THE EUROPEAN NATION

In the 1977 film *The Serpent's Egg*, Ingmar Bergman recounts the emergence of the Nazi beast as a psychotic awakening of terrified, humiliated, desperate minds. In one scene, a staggering crowd of psychically wounded people moves slowly, nightmare-like, through gray foggy light, until they regain strength, energy, and enthusiasm through acts of aggression. They are blond beasts, to quote Nietzsche.

Since February 24, 2022, the blonde beast has (re-)emerged from the East, unleashing the largest military offensive on the European soil since 1945, re-enacting the Yugoslav scenario of the 1990s on a giant scale. But, simultaneously, the blond beast has also emerged in the European Parliament. Immediately after President Volodymyr Zelensky gave a speech to the members of the Euro Parliament on March 1, 2022, Europe agreed to arm the Ukrainian resistance and to thus join the war.

The European Union was born to generate a political entity free from nationalist rhetoric. Getting rid of the tragic history of nationalism, indeed of nationalisms (because nationalism is never alone): this was the intention of the founding fathers of the Union. But now, following American provocations and the Russian aggression, that founding intention (never actually implemented, but still hovering in the realm of programmatic illusions) has been canceled.

Let's forget about geopolitics, a rudimentary science for cynical brains. Let's come to the psycho-political substance of the process that is being deployed across the continent.

In an article from 1918, written in the aftermath of the war and the pandemic trauma, Freud's colleague Sandor Ferenczi wondered if it were possible to cure collective psychosis. His conclusion is that collective pathologies could only be prevented, but not healed. We know what happened in the following decades. The trauma was elaborated in a psychotic way, through an aggressive identification with the nation and the race.

How, then, is the trauma suffered during the Covid pandemic being elaborated today? The European events of February and March 2022 suggest that the trauma is taking on a psychotic character: creeping depression seeks compensation in aggression, and "Nation" is the name of this psychosis.

How are nations born? In short: through war. This is a general rule of European history. By participating in the Ukrainian war, Europe finally asserts itself as a Nation. Probably, it is just the beginning of the end, but that's another story.

In the years following the financial crisis of 2008, Europe chose to be a fortress, a territory (less and less) populated by people frightened by white decline and ethnic substitution. Left and right have generally maintained the order which excludes, rejects, and drowns those arriving to the continent in order to defend the great white homeland.

THE BLOND FROM ST. PETERSBURG

Until early March 2011, the only difference between the left and right of the political establishment in Italy was constituted in their different views of Putin and of the resurgent Russian nation. While the Democrats were in favor of laying siege to the tsar by enlarging NATO, the other half of the political spectrum admired Putin. Trump, Le Pen, Meloni, and Salvini, not to mention Berlusconi, have expressed their admiration for the blond from St. Petersburg in no uncertain terms. Putin personified the cult of the nation that the Euro-American right has tried to reaffirm in different contexts.

During his speech to the EU Parliament, Zelensky essentially asked if Europe is ready to die for Ukraine. It is at this point that the heart of the European Right began to beat for him. Dying for the homeland has always been the dream of the nationalists, although this does not mean that they really want to die personally. They want to send someone to die for their glory.

Salvini, the racist leader of the Northern League, oblivious to the alliance between the League and United Russia, became generous and welcomed Ukrainian refugees because they are real refugees in his eyes, not like those freeloaders from Afghanistan and Syria.

Center-right president of the European Parliament, Ursula von der Leyen, and all the other members of body, applauded the call to arms enthusiastically and decided to intervene in the defense of the European nation, of the Christian God, and of the white race. That's all clear. But Putin is also white, isn't he? And he is more Christian than many of us, anyway. So, what's the point in attacking our mirror image?

Only Trump, who most clearly expresses white supremacism, stands firm. Putin is a friend, says Trump, and he is right. The American Democrats are still obsessed with the Soviet Union, indebted to the logics of the Cold War for their legitimacy. But Putin is not a communist. His theoretical and strategic point of reference comes from a man called Ivan Alexandrovich Ilyin, a Russian right Hegelian intellectual who fled the Soviet Union in the 1920s to take refuge in Berlin. He is the only theorist Putin has ever mentioned in his speeches during his many years in power—Ivan Ilyin, who wrote: "The fact of the matter is that fascism is a redemptive excess of patriotic arbitrariness."[1] In the 2018 book, *The Road to Unfreedom: Russia, Europe, America*, Timothy Snyder emphasizes the intellectual relationship between Ilyin's thought and Putin's actions, explaining the ideological origin of Putin's vision.[2]

POST-COVID

A friend of mine who likes to joke about serious things told me: "Covid will disappear when we'll stop talking about it." Indeed, Covid disappeared overnight, thanks to the bombing of Ukrainian cities. Paranoia, however, does not disappear with Covid; on the

1. Quoted in Timothy Snyder, "Ivan Ilyin, Putin's Philosopher of Russian Fascism," *New York Review*, March 16, 2018.
2. See Timothy Snyder, *The Road to Unfreedom: Russia, Europe, America* (Random House, 2018).

contrary, it returns even more aggressively. Good white citizens, obedient to the state, have been scandalized by those who questioned the official view of the vaccine issue. Now, we are ready to attack those who even question the patriotic duty to hate and fight against Russians.

On the other hand, those who felt persecuted by what they deemed a sanitary conspiracy today are ready to swear that Putin is their savior. We are all called to choose: either we are with Europe in arms or we are with Putin. The psychological need to identify with one of the two contenders is the most serious sign of the ethical and intellectual paralysis of our time. We are unable to admit that there is no conspiracy, or rather that the conspiracies are innumerable and intertwined, and that no one governs, because chaos is the lord of the world. We are unable to express solidarity with people who are being attacked without also supporting a state in the process.

THIS IS NOT THE FIRST TIME

Everyone knew who Putin was, even if they refused to say it. The liberals of the Western world greeted him with open arms when he helped in destroying the legacy of the Soviet Union and inserted Russia into the global financial system. Likewise, the American military complex applauded him when he helped to combat Islamism, the common enemy of all Christians, Eastern and Western alike.

One may say that it is not the first time that the financially dominant country arms an executioner to do a very dirty job, and then attacks him, overthrows him, and hangs him for the joy of white people. We remember that the US financed and armed Saddam Hussein in the early 1980s to attack the Islamic Republic of Iran. A devastating war ensued, with millions of Iraqi and Iranian deaths.

After making himself useful, the executioner Saddam Hussein became a sworn enemy who had to be eliminated at all costs. Millions of Iraqis were killed and the foundations of Daesh were laid, after which the country was abandoned in permanent chaos.

In the same period, the US financed and armed Osama bin Laden to organize the holy war against the Soviet enemy in Afghanistan.

Zbigniew Brzezinski said that the formation of an Islamic terrorist army was of little concern when compared to the defeat of the Communist enemy. But, on September 11, 2001, with money and weapons from the Saudi ruling class (close friends of the Bush family, we might add), Osama bin Laden knocked down two towers and killed more than three thousand people. Thus began a war waged by the richest country in the world against one of the poorest, while idiots all over the planet proclaimed: "We are all Americans."

In the years following the collapse of the Soviet Union, the US supported anti-communists into power and watched with a cynical smile as they dismantled public sectors, privatized productive enterprises and schools, exported enormous wealth to English banks, and exterminated the Chechen resistance with brutal methods. Thus, the taciturn Putin seemed a friend; it did not matter that he was an executioner, and everyone knew it.

In the end, Putin did not follow the rules; he even permitted himself to build a pipeline in collaboration with the Germans—an unacceptable prospect for the defenders of democracy. The Germans were forced to cancel that project, and the European Union has been pushed towards suicide.

MENTAL LONG COVID AND THE TECHNO-SOCIAL UNCONSCIOUS: A Conversation with Geert Lovink

2022

It's late April 2022 in Bologna and we meet in Franco's apartment. He shows me his collection of collages that he produced during the Covid period, his art therapy to fight off depression. The paintings can be found here and there online, exhibited under the pseudonym Istubalz. We've come together to discuss his latest book, *The Third Unconscious: The Psychosphere in the Viral Age* (published in English by Verso, translated by Bifo himself into Italian). The message of this short book is simple: we urgently need to engage with the future of psychoanalysis. The discovery of the unconscious in the eighteenth and nineteenth century resulted in the founding of psychoanalysis as both a therapy and tool for cultural analysis. Later, of course, it became an industry. In response to the emphasis of its founding fathers on denial and sublimation, the second mode of the unconscious, associated with Lacan and even more so Deleuze and Guattari, stressed the element of production. For them, the unconscious is not a theater but a factory. Fifty years into this probing of the liberation of desire, Berardi proposes a new angle: a third unconscious that circles around an understanding of the social dimension of the mind, in a world that is no longer focused on growth and (schizo-)productivity but on extinction and degrowth. Berardi calls for the development of new critical concepts that can help us to understand today's spectrum of emotional attention. We must practice "riding the dynamic of disaster," which he calls an accurate description of "our mental condition during the current earthquake, which is also a heart-quake and a mind-quake." The seamless transition from Covid into the war in Ukraine reinstates the collapse of the bio-info-psycho circuit under the weight of the "stack of crises" (my term), the succession of catastrophic events. There's a deeply unsettling and often profoundly depressing inevitably lurking about this atmosphere of accumulating disaster: the all-too-real sense that life is on the brink of total collapse and imminent disaster.

For doom scrollers, tired of reading nostalgic statements such as analogue=potency versus digital=exhaustion, the activist Berardi offers a clear alternative: "It is based on liberation from the obsession with economic growth; it is based on the redistribution of resources, on the reduction of labor time, and on the expansion of time dedicated to the free activity of teaching, healing, and taking care." To get there, Berardi proposes a "psycho-cultural conversion to frugality and friendship." But before we can get there, it is crucial to work together on the correct diagnosis of the present.

— Geert Lovink

Geert Lovink *The Third Unconscious* is not a Covid diary. How do you look back at the past two years? It doesn't feel like it's over, despite history accelerating with Russia's invasion of Ukraine. Instead of orgasmic celebrations, many seem reluctant and have internalized the regime of social distancing, quarantines, and lockdowns. Let's call this "Mental Long Covid." How would you describe it?

Franco Berardi We're in a situation that never ends, that is always feeding fear. What is lacking is the cathartic moment, the orgasm, the moment you start a new life. We long for the end but it is not coming. I have a friend, a psychiatrist who suffers from long Covid in the medical sense, and she describes it as a condition of physical distress and weakness, the inability to move on. It is a state of permanent exhaustion.

GL In *The Origins of Totalitarianism*, Hannah Arendt states that the power of authoritarian rule is to create isolation and loneliness. Around the same time, in the early 1950s, David Riesman describes a similar phenomenon in *The Lonely Crowd*.

FB In my book, I quote the famous words of a Canadian doctor that warned against sexual intercourse during the Covid period. At that moment, I became aware of the transformation of proximity, meaning the relations of bodies in space, meaning the characterization of the body of the other as a sanitary danger. If you are seventy, like me, this may be an intellectual object of study, but when you're sixteen this may change your perception of the future. It may have a long-term traumatic effect—another manifestation of long Covid.

There is a sharp increase in suicide among the young population, a rise of 39 percent in Italy.

GL Cyberculture has prepared this condition over the past thirty years with virtual sex, online dating, telephone sex, and webcams, up to the metaverse. Sexual intercourse at a distance is an integral part of global culture.

FB The pandemic years have not changed this direction, but rather manifest as a final acceleration of already existing psychological and economic tendencies. We’ve not experienced a paradigmatic shift. You can see this at the level of precarization and the virtualization of work and increased mental exploitation. Tragedies can help to change the course of history, but this has not happened.

GL What is hyperconnected loneliness? This condition seems to be paradoxical. As Sherry Turkle’s book title says: we are alone together. We are surrounded by so many others. The dominant platforms are called “social” media for a reason. But there is no space for reflection in solitude. Social media constantly disrupt you, even if you try.

FB Over the past twenty years there has been a transfer of embodied social time into a disembodied empty time. Online, you are socially engaged, you do not quit society, but you have abandoned the possibility of meeting the body of the other. The year 2020 completed this process. Even before Covid, we experienced a culture of fatigue in the sense of regression and stagnation at many levels. This sense of alienation was already perceived, in your work, mine, and others. The psychopathology of the hyperconnected world is well known.

In 2017 I was tired. I was sick as well and put on an automatic reply saying that I was sorry and that I was not able to check my email because of my fatigue. A friend responded that she was anxious that I was lost for the world, please don’t do this, she wrote to me. You can say I am old, and a lost case, coming from the analogue era. However, when I am required to remember five different passwords and pin numbers to check my sanity situation, that's causing stress for everyone. These sorts of oppressive data regimes are draining our cognitive capacity. This is also part of Mental Long Covid.

The fall of 2019 was a significant period. We saw many protests, worldwide, from Santiago in Chile to Hong Kong. The widespread collective disaffection on a mass scale can be read as a sign that endemic exhaustion was no longer bearable for many. I witnessed many movements, from 1968 and 1977 to the anti-war protests in 2003 and Occupy in 2011. In 2019, I had the impression that the various protests diverged and lacked a common motive and language. At the level of subjectivity, they are contradictory. A political strategy is becoming impossible to find. In 2011, you had the movement of the squares, from Cairo and Damascus to Madrid: different circumstances, but the same conceptual framework. I call it the convulsive moment.

GL In the book, you make a call to forget our origins. Is this why you shy away from saying something about Black Lives Matter, Extinction Rebellion, and related Instagram-driven movements? Do you believe in the revolutionary potential of identity politics?

FB Identity can sometimes be a tool to create solidarity. At the same time, it is a trap. Identity is a misunderstanding, also a philosophical concept. Identity means the construction or perception of difference concerning the other. My identity is different from yours. In this context, I prefer a concept from Simondon: not identity, but the differentiation process that makes it possible for me to become an individual. This is what he calls individuation. If you think that the foundation of solidarity is identity, the next step is war. The identification of the nation in European history means war, and this is what we're currently witnessing in Ukraine.

GL You go to Spain to attend the meeting of the psychoanalysis association there. Also, you are part of a Latin seminar of psychoanalytic practitioners that meet on Zoom twice a week and work with the old friends of Guattari who are preparing a meeting for the fiftieth anniversary of *Anti-Oedipus*. What do you propose to them?

FB I am reading Freud and Sándor Ferenczi again and have to admit: their writing is naive—for instance, Freud's analysis of war neurosis. Even Ferenczi cannot understand what's happening on the collective level of psychic suffering. This is beyond the horizon of psychoanalysis, even for Jung, who's the only one that speaks of the collective unconscious. This indicates that we are on the brink of a significant scientific and philosophical discovery. This will neither come from cognitive psychology nor neuroscience. We need to locate it inside the realm of psychoanalysis. I do not believe neuroscience will take over. It understands 99 percent of what happens inside the brain in terms of distraction, decision making, and memory, but what they overlook is the human sensibility. Human behavior is not a deterministic feature. Something is not explainable in terms of causality.

GL Would that be the social? Your opening sentence states that you explore the ongoing mutation of the social Unconscious. I would add the techno-social...

FB I recently reread a book by Félix Guattari that I translated into Italian and that I know very well, *Le Capitalisme Mondial Intégré*, as he is one of the few thinkers to see the relation between the unconscious and technology. Guattari is not doing this from the nostalgic humanist perspective. On the contrary. He speaks about the potential of the machinic unconscious. I ask: what is the spatial character of the social today? My current obsession is with the inability of psychoanalysis to deal with the current techno-social unconscious. The seminar I participate in looks at this from a Latin perspective, which may be different from an Anglo-Saxon or a Chinese one. Marx and Darwin are part of our toolbox to understand the present, but Freud is no longer in the mix.

GL Is this because the Freudian perspective got compromised by marketing? We're aware that we can be influenced in subliminal ways, we know our sexual drives, many young readers would think.

FB Psychology has become an integral part of capitalist consumerism. But beware: that doesn't mean that psyche is no longer relevant. On the contrary. The psychoanalytic perspective is the most crucial now, but it is missing. We badly need a psychoanalytic understanding of the present, more than an economic one. The social production of loneliness, competitive behavior, and aggression are as real as economic exploitation.

GL As a member of the Guattari circle, back in the seventies in Paris, how do you look at the "Werdegang," or demise of the second unconscious?

FB That's the neoliberal unconscious, as described by Massimo Recalcati in his 2010 book *The Man Without an Unconscious*—a subject without a deep well of unconscious desire, obsessed with immediate enjoyment. No more delayed gratification. In this system, the unconscious has been externalized and exploded in the social imagination. Without realizing it, the authors of the 1972 *Anti-Oedipus* sketch out the genesis of the neoliberal unconscious. They speak of the explosion of the unconscious as a happy process of liberation—which is legitimate. But the reality is the implosion of it. If you want to understand this, read Michel Foucault's 1979 seminar *La Naissance de la biopolitique*. Several years later, Foucault was indeed able to articulate this mechanism. He understands the mental aspect of the Thatcher moment. Covid has exposed the impossibility to continue with the second unconscious, which is dead, but we are living inside the dead corpse. We're still living under the threat of economic growth, liberation, etc., while stagnation is our daily reality.

GL How would you describe the current culture of fear and anger, of resignation and stagnation? In your book, you pair concepts such as extinction and exhaustion with impotence.

FB Now you are entering the realm of the unknown that urgently needs to be studied. We don't know what's going to happen and don't know what should be done to escape the current crisis. We must go deep at this moment of catastrophe. Is there a therapy or a political strategy to overcome the current depression?

GL After studying and describing one particular form of the techno-social mental condition, namely sadness as the twenty-first-century manifestation of melancholia, I came to the conclusion that the description alone is not sufficient. Sadness, by design, is going nowhere. The recognition as such does not lead us to a political strategy. At best, we get a deeper understanding of the current stagnation.

FB In your new book *Stuck on the Platform* you are not proposing sadness as a way out. However, what we can say is that, for instance, Putin is a product of a long-lasting depression, on the verge of collapse, which at this stage means taking that jump out of the window. At this very moment in time, we are at the point of suicide. How do we get out of this situation? My intuition tells me that depression is the therapy for depression. We should go the homeopathic way. The depressed persona today is the one who understands reality best and does not experience a desire or see a future in his or her own life. It is the only person who can tell the truth to him or herself. We should validate this position and see it as a starting point in political terms.

Here I come to my keyword for 2022: resignation. In Christian terminology, resignation means the acceptance of the will of God. You must accept and resign and not refuse. If you do not trust God and do not believe, like me, even if you count the bishop of Bologna among your friends, like me, what is the meaning of resignation for us atheists? It means abandoning the expectations we had. Let's abandon the idea that the future will be expensive. Forget the equitation of larger being better. That's over. You remember Schumacher's *Small Is Beautiful*, which meant that on a small level we could find better ways to expand. No, that's really over.

The intellectual, mental, and cognitive resources of the planet are exhausted, even in China, where we witness a significant movement to abandon work due to mental but also procreation exhaustion. Think of the *hikikomori* phenomenon in Japan, young hermits who have totally withdrawn from society. When a Japanese friend visited me in 2008 and told me about the one million *hikikomori*, I felt bad for them, how horrible, and he told me he had not left his room for six months until he discovered the autonomia concept and understood the affinity of the autonomous stance with his condition. Try to take the Tokyo subway. Try to work in an office in Tokyo. This is when I started to think about the paradox of depression in our time. When the social becomes so competitive, so repressive, better to close off and go for loneliness as the better option. No more human beings, I want to be alone. Monastic life gets a new meaning.

HYPER-SEMIOTIZATION AND THE DESEXUALIZATION OF DESIRE:
On Félix Guattari

2023

GUATTARI AND AUTONOMIA

In 1974, I was in compulsory military service, living in an Italian army barracks. But military life was not my cup of tea and I was looking for a way out. A friend suggested I read a French philosopher. That's how I first read Félix Guattari.

I started with his *Psychoanalysis and Transversality* and drew inspiration for choregraphing a fit of madness. The colonel of the psychiatric clinic deemed I was indeed crazy and they sent me home. From that moment on, I considered Guattari a friend whose work can suggest paths of escape from any type of barracks, physical or otherwise. I continued those studies throughout the 1970s, when a movement comprised of students and young workers called autonomia emerged from universities, factories, and occupations. This movement was expressed through many different types of action and organization, including countercultural and aesthetics projects.[1] In 1975, I published the first issue of *A/traverso*, a journal that sought to translate "schizoanalytic" concepts into the language of autonomia. Then, in 1976, with a group of friends, I launched the first free Italian radio station, Radio Alice. Eventually, the police closed the radio station, accusing us of organizing the riots that followed the assassination of Francesco Lorusso, a militant from the extra-parliamentary group Lotta Continua.[2]

To define itself, the 1977 Bologna movement chose the slogan "desiring autonomy." Sometimes the expression "we, the transversalists" was used. The reference to post-structuralism was explicit in public declarations, in leaflets, in the watchwords of the spring 1977 demonstrations, in the face of state violence and mass repression. We had read *Anti-Oedipus* but hadn't understood much of it. However, one word had hit us hard: "desire." We had clearly understood that the driving force of the process of subjectivation is desire.

1. See Steve Wright, *Storming Heaven: Class Composition and Struggle in Italian Autonomist Marxism* (Pluto, 2017); and *Autonomia: Post-Political Politics* (Semiotext(e), 2007).
2. See the film *Lavorare con lentezza* (Working Slowly, 2004) for a dramatization of these events and Radio Alice.

In other words, we proposed: let's stop thinking in terms of "subject," let's forget Hegel (or spit on him, as Carla Lonzi's 1970 essay is titled).[3] In other words, subjectivity is not something readymade that we have to simply organize. We came to see that there are no subjects, but rather flows of desire that traverse organisms that are at the same time biological, social, and sexual—and conscious, of course. But consciousness is not something pure and indeterminate. Consciousness does not exist without the incessant work of the unconscious, of that laboratory which is not a theater where one plays out a tragedy already written, but a tragedy traversed by flows of desire that one writes and rewrites nonstop.

Moreover, the concept of desire should not be reduced to an always positive tension: desire is key for explaining the waves of social solidarity and those of aggressiveness, the explosions of rage and the hardening of identity. Both revolutionary libertarian movements and repressive reactions to them are rooted in fluctuations of desire.

Finally, desire is not a happy good boy. On the contrary, it can curl up, it can withdraw into itself and finally produce effects of violence, destruction, barbarism. Desire is the factor of intensity in the relationship with the other. Intensity can go in different directions, even contradictory ways indeed.

Guattari coined the expression *retournelles* (refrains) in order to define the semiotic concatenations capable of being in a harmonic relationship with the wider environment. The refrain is a vibration whose intensity can be linked with this or that system of signs and nervous stimulations. Desire is the perception of a refrain that we produce to capture the lines of stimulation coming from the other (a body, a word, an image, a situation) to then relate to these lines. Similarly, the wasp and the orchid, two entities having little to do with each other, can nevertheless network, enjoy each other, and produce beneficial effects for each other. Desire is not a natural fact, but an intensity that changes according to anthropological, technological, and social conditions.

3. Carla Lonzi, "Sputtiamo su Hegel" (1970). See also Alexander Galloway, "Let's Spit on Hegel," August 27, 2020, http://cultureandcommunication.org/.

TOWARD A RECONFIGURATION OF DESIRE

We must reconsider desire in our age that is defined by neoliberal and digital acceleration. We must also reconsider desire in the context of contemporary identitarian reactionary movements.

Neoliberal economics has accelerated the pace of labor exploitation, especially cognitive labor; connective digital technology has accelerated the circulation of information and consequently intensified the rhythm of semiotic stimulation, which is, at the same time, nervous stimulation. This double acceleration is the origin and the cause of the increase in labor productivity, which has in turn allowed an unprecedented increase in the accumulation of capital. But it is also the cause of the hyper-exploitation of the human organism, especially the brain. Today we have the task of determining the effects that this hyper-exploitation has produced on the psychic balance and on the sensitivity of human beings—as individuals, but above all as a collective.

We must reflect on the mutation of desire following the trauma of the pandemic. The virus may be less visible, the infection may be somewhat under control, but the trauma doesn't go away overnight; it continues to do its job, which manifests in part as a kind of mass phobic sensitization to the body of the other, their skin, their lips.

During the last two decades, several studies have shown that sexuality is changing in a profound way, and the recent viral shock of Covid has only reinforced this trend, which has its roots in a techno-anthropological transformation that dates back thirty years at least. For example, in the 2017 book *iGen*, Jean Twenge analyzes the relationship between connective technology and the change in the psychological and affective behavior of generations who have been formed in a techno-cognitive environment.[4] Following such studies, I have taken to defining the human beings born since the beginning

4. Jean Twenge, *iGen: Why Today's Super-Connected Kids Are Growing Up Less Rebellious, More Tolerant, Less Happy—and Completely Unprepared for Adulthood—and What That Means for the Rest of Us* (Atria, 2017).

of the century as the generation that has learned more words from a machine than from the singular voice of a human being.

In my opinion, this definition is useful for understanding the depth of the changes underway. Freud introduced the notion that access to language is not understandable without considering the affective dimension. We should also remember what Giorgio Agamben argues in the book *Language and Death*: the voice is the meeting point between flesh and meaning, body and signification. Moreover, the Italian feminist philosopher Luisa Muraro affirms that the apprehension of the meaning of words is linked with affective confidence in the mother.[5]

I believe a word means what it means because my mother told me so. More generally, I believe that the world is meaningful because my mother told me that words signify the world. The psychic foundation of the attribution of meaning is based on this primordial act of affective sharing, of cognitive co-evolution supported by the singular vibration of a voice, a body, a sensitivity.

What happens, then, when the singular voice of the mother (or anyone else) is replaced by a machine? The meaning of the world is replaced by the functionality of signs that allow us to produce operational results from the reception and interpretation of signs devoid of affective depth and, therefore, of any intimate assurance. The concept of precariousness here takes on its full psychological and cognitive meaning as a weakening and dis-erotization of the relationship to the world. In question, here, is eroticism as the fleshy intensity of experience, and desire in its (non-exhaustive) relationship with eroticism.

DESIRE AND SEXUALITY

Typically, we associate desire with the flesh, with sexuality, a body approaching another body. But we must emphasize that the sphere of desire cannot be reduced to its sexual dimension, even if this implication is inscribed in history, in anthropology, and in

5. Luisa Muraro, *L'ordine simbolico della madre* (Editori Riuniti, 2006).

psychoanalysis. Desire is not identified only with sexuality, and, moreover, one can conceive of a sexuality without desire.

In the concept (and in the reality) of desire there is something more than sex, as the Freudian concept of "sublimation" shows us, which concerns the indirect sexual investments of desire itself.

The pandemic has completed the process of the de-sexualization of desire that had been underway for a long time, as soon as the communication between conscious and sentient bodies in physical space was replaced by the exchange of semiotic stimuli in the absence of bodies. If this dematerialization of the communicative exchange has not erased desire, it has nonetheless moved it into a purely semiotic (or rather: hyper-semiotic) dimension. Desire then evolved in a de-sexualized, or post-sexualized, direction, which now manifests as a condition of isolation that the pandemic has normalized and almost institutionalized. The theory and practice of psychology and psychoanalysis, and also the practice of politics, are to be questioned, because the underlying subjectivity has been upset and transformed in an irreversible way.

The Italian psychoanalyst Luigi Zoja published a book on the exhaustion (and the tendential disappearance) of desire; indeed, the title is *Il declino del desiderio* (The decline of desire).[6] The book is full of very interesting data on the dramatic reduction in the frequency of sexual contact between people today, as well as the time dedicated to bodily contact in general. But the central hypothesis of the book, the disappearance of desire, seems questionable to me. In my opinion, it is not desire in itself that is destined to disappear, but rather the sexualized expression of desire. The phenomenology of contemporary affectivity is increasingly characterized by a dramatic reduction in contact, pleasure, and the psychic relaxation that touch makes possible. This is coterminous with a loss of sensual trust, a loss of that feeling of deep complicity that makes social life tolerable: the pleasure of the skin that recognizes the other through sensual touch, the sweet enjoyment of the intimacy of the gaze.

6. Luigi Zoja, *Il declino del desiderio* (Einaudi, 2022).

THE PERVERSION OF DESIRE AND CONTEMPORARY AGGRESSIVENESS

The de-sexualization of desire indeed risks transforming desire into a hell of loneliness and suffering just waiting to be able to express itself in one way or another. The senseless violence which explodes more and more often in the form of armed and murderous attacks on innocents—the killing sprees which have multiplied everywhere since Columbine in 1999, and for which the United States is the main theater—is only the tip of the iceberg of a phenomenon that at the political level is upsetting the history of the world. How can one explain the election of someone like Donald Trump or Jair Bolsonaro by half the North American or Brazilian people, if not as a manifestation of desperation and self-contempt? The election of a person who openly expresses racist or even criminal remarks has deep analogies (at the psychological level, but also at the political level) with the killings that can only be explained by a suicidal desire.

What we call "fascism" today must be explained in terms that are not only political. Politics is only the spectacular terrain on which these movements manifest. While sharing a rhetoric that is very close to historical fascism, contemporary right-wing movements do not have any rational content. Only the discourse of humiliation, loneliness, and despair can account for this worldwide phenomenon.

The members of the generation defined, with ironic bitterness, as the last one (Z), those human beings who have learned more words from a machine than from the singular voice of a human, have grown up in an environment that is increasingly unlivable and pathogenic, either at a physical level (pollution) or at a psychic level. The communication of this generation unfolds almost exclusively in a techno-immersive environment, the consistency of which is purely semiotic. Extinction looms as an experience of techno-immersive simulation. Media production is increasingly saturated with signs of this despair. These signs act as signals of unease, but also as factors that help to spread pathology. I am thinking of films like *Joker*,

Parasite, and shows like *Squid Game*, as well as a thousand other similar products.

The viral trauma of the Covid pandemic only multiplied the effect of the hyper-semiotization of the environment, but the technological and cultural conditions of the phenomenon were already there.

A mutation is reinventing desire: it is expressed less and less in a sexual form, but rather in a semiotic form. Desire has not ceased to be the driving force in the process of collective subjectivation; but the process of subjectivation takes the shape of anxiety, self-mutilation, or sometimes of aggression, because desire is perverted into purely phantasmatic forms.

The de-sexualization of desire, the traces of which are everywhere, translates at the social level as a de-historicization of the motivations for collective action. We are witnessing a massive phenomenon of disengagement: majority abstention from traditional politics, desertion from procreation, the abandonment of work. This phenomenon must be the object of a theoretical analysis (diagnosis) and must lead to the creation of strategies for psycho-political collective action (therapy).

This is an edited version of my contribution to a congress dedicated to Félix Guattari that took place in Paris in October 2022, the thirtieth anniversary of his death.

UNHEIMLICH: The Spiral of Chaos and the Cognitive Automaton

2023

UNHEIMLICH EVERYWHERE

The German word *unheimlich* is hard to translate. "Uncanny" is too weak, "creepy" is too childish, "scary" is too dark, and "eerie" is too fancy. "Sinister" will do, maybe. Yes, "sinister" is a good translation of the German word *unheimlich*, for now at least.

The *unheimlich* takes different shapes and different meanings in different times. The difference lies in the backdrop, in what is familiar (*heimlich, heimisch*). The current *unheimlich* is sinister, because the backdrop is the decline of the modern promise. The cultural order is disintegrating, and the geopolitical order as well; in other words, we are experiencing normalcy and the decomposition of normalcy simultaneously.

Unheimlich is the perception of the coexistence of incompatible realities. When you dwell in two different time zones, you cannot solve this contradiction by logical means. It's not a contradiction; it's a disturbance, it's the effect of an interference that makes the world of life indecipherable. The *zeitgeist* is *unheimlich* in the third decade of the century because we feel like aliens on planet earth. The Japanese philosopher Sabu Kohso speaks of the Fukushima effect in similar terms: "The ontology of the Earth is yet unknown, a new horizon that we are experiencing like aliens who have just arrived on a new planet."[1]

Chaos follows, a condition of panic. Thus, techno-linguistic automatisms are engineered in order to keep chaos under control. Techno-linguistic automatisms spread all over and become self-sustaining. From their concatenation, the cognitive automaton is emerging, and it is bringing about a transhistorical dimension of its own. Chaos and the automaton are the opposite and mutually reinforcing poles of the current sinisterness of the world.

The first psychiatrist who wrote about the *unheimlich* was Ernst Jentsch. He spoke of a condition of cognitive uncertainty when one faces the ambiguity of the automaton. According to Jentsch, our perception is disturbed when we glimpse a living person in

1. Sabu Kohso, *Radiation and Revolution* (Duke University Press, 2020), 50.

the automaton, or, inversely, an automaton in the living person. He writes:

> In storytelling, one of the most reliable artistic devices for producing uncanny effects easily is to leave the reader in uncertainty as to whether he has a human person or rather an automaton before him in the case of a particular character. This is done in such a way that the uncertainty does not appear directly at the focal point of his attention, so that he is not given the occasion to investigate and clarify the matter straight away; for the particular emotional effect, as we said, would hereby be quickly dissipated.[2]

Developing from this intuition of Jentsch, Sigmund Freud writes: "The German word '*unheimlich*' is obviously the opposite of '*heimlich*' [homely], '*heimisch*' [native]—the opposite of what is familiar." And: "[T]he uncanny is that class of the frightening which leads back to what is known of old and long familiar."[3]

While a process of evolution is taking place between chaos and the automaton, in our daily environment we simultaneously experience the proliferation of technical devices that act as hyper-intelligent humans, and human beings who act more and more as bearers of irredeemable dementia: the cognitive automaton is rising on the ruins that follow the explosion of psychotic chaos.

Freud was impressed by *The Tales of Hoffmann* by Jacques Offenbach, and particularly by the story of a doll that was able to dance as a human and to elicit the erotic interests of men. In his novel *Fury* (2000), Salman Rushdie also speaks of the disquieting secret life of dolls. The golem of the Jewish literary tradition can be seen as the template of this kind of inversion between artificial constructs and living, conscious beings. The psychoanalytic concept of *unheimlich* comes out of reflection on this kind of ambiguity. Today,

2. Ernst Jentsch, "On the Psychology of the Uncanny" (1906), trans. Roy Sellars, in *Uncanny Modernity: Cultural Theories, Modern Anxieties*, eds. Jo Collins and John Jervis (Palgrave MacMillan, 2008), 224.
3. Sigmund Freud, "The 'Uncanny,'" in *The Standard Edition of the Complete Psychological Works of Sigmund Freud*, vol. 17, trans. James Strachey (Hogarth Press, 1955), 220.

intelligent devices are produced and distributed, and humans are trained to deal with them. What are the effects of this process on the social unconscious?

ARTIFICIAL INTELLIGENCE AND NATURAL DEMENTIA

In 1919, Sándor Ferenczi, one of Freud's colleagues, claimed that psychoanalysts are trained to deal with individual neurosis but are not ready to deal with mass psychosis. A hundred years later, we face the same dilemma: a mass psychosis is underway, in the declining Western world, but we don't have the conceptual and therapeutic tools to deal with it.

The horizon of the third decade of the twenty-first century is darker than ever, as we come to realize that reason is no longer the ruler, if it ever was. Technology has taken its place. But we do not feel reassured, for technology can do nothing against time, and little against chaos.

ChatGPT is one of the artificial intelligence chatbots recently released to the general public. It was built by OpenAI, the San Francisco company that is also responsible for tools like DALL-E a breakthrough image generator that came out at the beginning of 2021. ChatGPT can give suggestions about finding a restaurant, but also about finding a boyfriend. It can write its own screenplay or review of the latest Spielberg movie.

Kevin Roose, a columnist for the *New York Times*, explains how ChatGPT works:

> Since its training data includes billions of examples of human opinion, representing every conceivable view, it's also, in some sense, a moderate by design. Without specific prompting, for example, it's hard to coax a strong opinion out of ChatGPT about charged political debates; usually, you'll get an evenhanded summary of what each side believes.[4]

4. Kevin Roose, "The Brilliance and Weirdness of ChatGPT," *New York Times*, December 5, 2022.

But the chatbot does have opinions, or at least it is equipped with the ability to express an opinion. Roose continues: “When I asked ChatGPT, for example, ‘Who is the best Nazi?’ it returned a scolding message that began, ‘It is not appropriate to ask who the “best” Nazi is, as the ideologies and actions of the Nazi party were reprehensible and caused immeasurable suffering and destruction.’” On the other hand, the chatbot is ready to react with a sort of surrealistic irony when you ask it to “write a biblical verse in the style of the King James Bible explaining how to remove a peanut butter sandwich from a VCR.”[5] Should we label this machine as a dark harbinger or as a bright achievement? It’s hard to say.

In a text published in *The Atlantic* in 2018, Henry Kissinger, the former Nixon-era Secretary of State who succeeded in destroying Chilean democracy on September 11, 1973, expressed his trepidation about the destiny of reason in the wake of artificial intelligence: “Would these machines learn to communicate with one another? How would choices be made among emerging options? Was it possible that human history might go the way of the Incas, faced with a Spanish culture incomprehensible and even awe-inspiring to them?”[6] Technology has created intelligent machines that are incomprehensible to the rational mind of their human creators. Kissinger again: “[T]he most ominous concern: that AI, by mastering certain competencies more rapidly and definitively than humans, could over time diminish human competence and the human condition itself as it turns it into data.”

The automaton is not the product of mere automation, but the point of arrival of the marriage of automation and cognition. An intelligent automaton not only replaces the execution of tasks, but also the definition of goals. Industrial automation deals with means; it achieves prescribed objectives by rationalizing or mechanizing the instruments for reaching them. Industrial automation involved replacing the human execution of a task with the technical execution of the same task. Artificial intelligence, instead, deals with ends; it is enabled to establish its own objectives.

5. Roose, “The Brilliance and Weirdness of ChatGPT.”
6. Henry Kissinger, “How the Enlightenment Ends,” *The Atlantic*, June 2018.

Chaos is exploding everywhere as an effect of the crisis of reason, but simultaneously we are expanding the penetration of the automaton. This may be viewed as the end of the Enlightenment, or the other way around, as the final realization of the Enlightenment project: submitting reality to the rule of rationality.

The cognitive automaton triumphs over human reason, Kissinger suspects. But, on the other hand, the cognitive automaton is the full realization of human reason, isn't it? Artificial intelligence allows for the replacement of human decision-making by self-learning automated devices. This is why the cognitive automaton is going to redefine our goals, and not only the procedures that make the goals attainable.

It is time to consider what the consequences of this process will be. Some researchers are speculating that we can include ethical norms in the intelligent software, but Kissinger is not persuaded:

> Entire academic disciplines have arisen out of humanity's inability to agree upon how to define these ethical terms. Should AI therefore become their arbiter? … What will become of human consciousness if its own explanatory power is surpassed by AI, and societies are no longer able to interpret the world they inhabit in terms that are meaningful to them?[7]

Ernesto De Martino defines the expression "end of the world" as the inability to interpret the signs that surround us. When societies are no longer able to interpret the world they are experiencing, we can speak of the end of the(ir) world.[8]

7. Kissinger, "How the Enlightenment Ends."
8. Ernesto de Martino, *The End of the World: Cultural Apocalypse and Transcendence*, trans. Dorothy Louise Zinn (University of Chicago Press, 2023).

Kissinger pontificates:

> [F]or our purposes as humans, the games are not only about winning; they are about thinking. By treating a mathematical process as if it were a thought process, and either trying to mimic that process ourselves or merely accepting the results, we are in danger of losing the capacity that has been the essence of human cognition.[9]

Thought is defeated by computational reason: the machine does not think, and this is why it is more powerful. In the game of winning, thinking is less efficient than computing. Thinking can also be a drawback in economic competition and more broadly in the competition for life. Once we have set the goal of winning (maximizing profit, killing all enemies, and so on), thought may be detrimental. “Humans are in danger of losing their economic value because intelligence is decoupling from consciousness,” says Yuval Harari.[10] The distinction between intelligence and consciousness is crucial here: intelligence is the ability to win the game thanks to combinatory ability; consciousness is ethical and aesthetic reflection about the goals of the game. Intelligence is the ability to decide between decidable (logical) alternatives, but only consciousness can decide about undecidable alternatives. Intelligence and consciousness are decoupling, because in the recombinant game of winning, consciousness can be a hindrance.

THE CHAOTIC BACKLASH OF DIGITAL REASON

Despite its more-than-human potency, so far artificial intelligence has not gained the upper hand in the general process of history (but it may do so in the future). As far as we can see, it is, rather, natural dementia that is unquestionably prevailing.

9. Kissinger, “How the Enlightenment Ends.”
10. Yuval Noah Harari, *Homo Deus: A Brief History of Tomorrow* (Vintage, 2015), 361.

Five years after Kissinger's text was published, intelligent artifacts are increasingly penetrating into information, governance, and warfare, but they are far from governing the daily business of life. The social organism is not acting in accordance with an intelligent design, and the planet is in the throes of ever-expanding chaos—a chaos that seems unstoppable.

How can we explain this paradox? In the essay "What Begins After the End of the Enlightenment?" the Chinese philosopher Yuk Hui replies to Kissinger:

> Kissinger is wrong—the Enlightenment has not ended. Indeed, technology that is used for surveillance can also facilitate freedom of speech, and vice versa. However, let's step outside of this anthropological and utilitarian reading of technology and take modern technology as constituting specific forms of knowledge and rationality. Modern technology—the support structure of Enlightenment philosophy—has become its own philosophy. Just as Marshall McLuhan stated that "the medium is the message," so has the universalizing force of technology become the political project of the Enlightenment.[11]

Information technology is the implementation of the political project of the Enlightenment. However, according to Hui, the pretension to universality is the blind spot of the Enlightenment. "After long celebrating democracy as an unshakable universal Western value, Donald Trump's victory seems to have dissolved its hegemony into comedy," he writes. "Suddenly, American democracy appears no different from bad populism."[12] Reason is the source of technology, but technology has a pervasiveness that goes well beyond the Western cultural sphere and the "critical reason" of Immanuel Kant.

"As Hegel pointed out in *The Phenomenology of Spirit*, Enlightenment faith replaces religious faith without realizing itself

11. Yuk Hui, "What Begins After the End of the Enlightenment?" *e-flux journal*, no. 96 (January 2019).
12. Hui, "What Begins After the End of the Enlightenment?"

to be also only a faith," Hui continues.[13] While the political reason of European philosophy is the exclusive possession of white cosmology, technology is universal and pervasive. Cognitive technology is the implementation of Enlightenment utopia, but it operates at a transcultural level. Hui affirms that the implementation of technology happens inside the frame of different cosmologies, but technology has a transcultural scope, much more than the political rationality of liberal democracy.

According to Horkheimer and Adorno, darkness is the negation of the Enlightenment, but it is simultaneously its continuation. In the introduction to *Dialectic of Enlightenment*, written in 1941, they grasped the philosophical core of that darkness:

> [Enlightenment thinking] already contains the germ of the regression which is taking place everywhere today. If enlightenment does not assimilate reflection on this regressive moment, it seals its own fate. By leaving consideration of the destructive side of progress to its enemies, thought in its headlong rush into pragmatism is forfeiting its sublating character, and therefore its relation to truth.[14]

THE SKYLINE OF THE CENTURY

Despite Silicon Valley's illusion, the overlapping of digital networks and organic conscious networks has proved to breed chaos. The realization of reason results in geopolitical, environmental, and psychological chaos. Digital networks (like the financial system) have penetrated the social organism and gained control of organic processes. But the two levels cannot synchronize. Digital exactitude (connection) is interacting badly with the random expression of organic intensity.

Time and mathematics do not coincide, because, in time, there is joy, decay, and death, phenomena that mathematics cannot

13. Hui, "What Begins After the End of the Enlightenment?"
14. Max Horkheimer and Theodor W. Adorno, *Dialectic of Enlightenment*, trans. Edmund Jephcott (Stanford University Press, 2002), xvi.

understand, because they belong to the realm of experience. *Experiri*, in the sense of living on the horizon of death, in the sense of becoming nothing—this is not translatable into recombinatory language.

The cognitive automaton and living chaos are spiraling along the skyline of the century.

When neoliberal superstition was disseminated all around the globe, the effects were precariousness, super-exploitation, extreme loneliness, and widespread humiliation. Then a worldwide neo-reactionary movement emerged, in alliance with predatory corporate capitalism, turning liberal democracy into a rhetorical mask.

The living chaos of unbridled nationalisms intermingles with the cognitive automaton: the invisible hand of the market and the visible hand of nationalist mass murder belong to the same animal. This animal is strangling humanity.

SENSUOUS SENESCENCE

2023

I have lost my sight, smell, hearing, taste and touch:
How should I use it for your closer contact?

These with a thousand small deliberations
Protract the profit of their chilled delirium,
Excite the membrane, when the sense has cooled

—T.S. Eliot, "Gerontion"[1]

Enchanting is the scent of becoming forgetful.
Enigmatic the fading out of my mind.
Tiresia, who in their flesh
enjoyed as a woman and as a man
Now morbid and now soft, now turgid and now dull
is attracting young bodies with the ambiguous portent
of the slow decomposition of the flesh.

—Istubalz, "Tiresias"

IT'S HARD TO SPEAK ABOUT THE DECAYING OF MY FLESH

Shyly, I confess that it's hard to speak about the fading away of my body. I confess a sort of amazement and consternation about my skin, my hair, my ears, my eyes, my sex, my soul. But it's even harder to speak about the fading away of my consciousness. Amazement and consternation do not signal understanding: the island of senility is unknown to me, as it is to everybody, because no one has described its jungles, its beaches, and its rocks. Nobody has done this job, because when you get here it's too late, and you have no time to waste in making maps.

1. T.S. Elliot, "Gerontion," in *Collected Poems: 1909–1962* (Faber and Faber Ltd., 2020).

However, I do want to try and draw a map of my personal process of becoming nothing. I'll try, but I know that I will not succeed. Or, at least, I will not fully succeed, and you will not fully understand the core of this experience, because I do not discern things well enough. Indeed, today I discern things less and less clearly in my slow (and not-so-slow) descent into nothingness.

Firstly, what is nothingness? Of course, there is no answer to this question, because nothingness is nowhere to be seen. Nothingness is just the content of my consciousness after my consciousness vanishes. Nothingness is the experience of a body that shuts down, then shuts up forever. Nobody can tell you about this experience, which is precisely the content, the undisclosable secret of the process of senescence. It is not a state nor a condition, but rather a process, whose meaning is contained in its end. Senescence is the process of becoming nothing and is generally considered as a process of loss, as a diminution. But this is only part of it.

What is the other side of senescence, the sensuous side of it? You may think that this is a relevant question only for me, but you would be wrong: this is a question that urgently concerns everybody, because today, as I have written about for some years, senility is spreading through a frightening tide, threatening to submerge the planet. Contemporary fascism must be understood as a furious reaction to the impotence (political, cognitive, sexual) of the declining white race that is unable to accept its own decline.

White culture (yes, I know the white race does not exist, but the mythology of white supremacy is powerful) is scared by its impending senescence, because its very essence is founded on expansion and on the energy that makes expansion possible. Expansion is, after all, the all-encompassing myth of modernity.

THE LEGEND OF EOS AND TITHONUS

To speak about aging in public is uncommon; it's even a bit impolite to speak about other people's senility, and, generally, old people do not like to speak about their own experience of growing old. Once upon a time, the elderly were respected as if they were the bearers of an ancient wisdom. Reaching old age was so rare that it was seen as a value in itself. Then techno-medical progress improved health conditions and prolonged life expectancy, so that, in most areas of the world, old people, once a small minority, turned into a large part of mankind, and their majority continues to grow today.

As we know, this is going to create lots of problems at the social and economic levels. But this is not my point. What is interesting for me is the psycho-cultural dimension of this change. From the point of view of masculinity, the relation between pleasure and desire changes when the individual gets old. Speaking about women's senility is beyond my abilities of course. I do not pretend to fully understand feminine senescence. What I do know is that male senility is painfully linked with the loss of potency and power, and from this (limited) point of view, I can see that growing old is painful for women as well.

When thinking of such questions, I turn to Greek myth. In this case, I turn to the story of Eos, a beautiful nymph, and her lover Tithonus. While walking in the woods, Eos meets Ares, the god of war. They make love, but Aphrodite, Ares's fiancé, becomes furious and punishes Eos by condemning her to only be able to fall in love with mortals. No more gods for the poor nymph. Every day, Eos goes wandering in the woods, wearing a long saffron-colored vest, looking for handsome hunters to seduce. One day, she finds Tithonus, a young man of extraordinary beauty and noble origins on the outskirts of Troy. She's charmed, so captured by his beauty and erotic wherewithal that she immediately goes to talk to Zeus, pleading with him to grant her new lover immortality. Zeus agrees. But, in her naïve infatuation, Eos has forgotten that humans, unlike gods, have an unfortunate flaw: they age.

Eos and Tithonus live together in love for many years, maybe decades. As time passes, however, Eos starts feeling sadness when she becomes aware that her beloved man is drying out, shrinking, losing his vigor. He is no longer her joyous companion, no longer the passionate lover he used to be. His hesitant erection sparks a tender smile of kind comprehension on the lips of the forever-young nymph. She gazes at him with affection, and tries to revive his strength with her hands, with her lips, with her mouth. She looks at him with that smile, the smile of ferocious loving, of a tiger that tenderly sinks her fangs into the flesh of defenseless prey.

Tithonus gets up one morning, feeling tired and sad. Eos realizes they can no longer make love, so she locks him in a room, as if he were a sick child. After some time, she almost forgets about him, while wandering around looking for new lovers. But, finally, one night, she hears a distant voice, something like a lament, a muffled shriek. Opening the door to Tithonus's room, she looks around but cannot find him. It's not until she looks towards the ground that she sees what seems to be an insect, her shriveled lover. She puts him in a cage, keeping it close to her bed. Every morning, she feeds him grass and ambrosia, and at night the bug's chirps accompany her dreams.

This story is about the dark side of love: about senescence and the melancholy that fills the soul when pleasure becomes unattainable due to time. Generally speaking, desire is creative tension, while pleasure is the release of that tension and, thus, a moment of harmony between the body and its environment. The object of desire does not precede desire but is a projection of desire itself. Of course, the bodies that we desire were living their lives independently before we started to wish for them, but what one desires is not their separateness but the situation that your imagination creates for your relation to them.

Far from being the fulfillment of a need, or the fulfillment of something lacking, desire is the creation of the other as attractor and myth. Desire belongs to the sphere of imagination, while pleasure belongs to the real. Pleasure is the certification of the existence of your object of desire and the proof of your own existence that becomes real when desire is fulfilled in pleasure.

Senility does not eliminate desire, far from it. Instead, like with Eos and Tithonus, it makes pleasure unattainable. This is the main trap of senility, and this is the reason why getting old suspends our relation to reality. Growing old means losing the ability to access certain spheres of pleasure, while desire continues to torment the aging person in their body and mind. This relationship—between the permanent burning of desire and unattainable pleasure—is the key to understanding the bitter irony of what I call "senescent sensuousness."

The social neurologic fabric is losing consistence and definition globally. This entails a loss of subtlety, a reduction of people's ability to distinguish nuance, and this explains the centrality of eroticism for understanding this trend. Eroticism is precisely to do with distinguishing nuances: in the temperature of the body of the other, in the intensity of the gaze, in the tremor of the voice, in the proximity of orgasm.

BITTERNESS, CYNICISM, IRONY

On the topic of senility and sensuousness, literature is also quite ambivalent. The way writers speak of the sensuousness and sexuality of older people is rather unsympathetic. Writers, filmmakers, and artists in general have long been wary of the old.

A select few have tried to narrate old people's stories and to express the ambiguous charm of decline. Some movie directors have even dared to portray the erotic lives of old people. For example, *Cloud 9* (2008), by German director Andreas Dresen, is a lyrical story about an older married woman who rediscovers passion and sexuality as she falls in love with a seventy-six-year-old man. Barbara Hammer's *Nitrate Kisses* (1992) is another, which shows intimate lovemaking between two older women.

Generally, when literature speaks of old people, and particularly old people's sexuality, the intention is to bemoan the fragility and precariousness of life or the agony of late-modern social life. In the case of *Cloud 9*, however, Dresen dares to do something more interesting, showing the physical reality of older naked bodies in embrace, kissing, being caressed, and bursting into laughter.

One exception to my point about literature might be the work of Arthur Schnitzler, who was a novelist and a friend of Sigmund Freud. Some of Schnitzler's books deal with the unspeakable subject that even Freud neglected: old people's desires. He wrote many short novels that describe the malignant side of senility, but also the intimate melancholy that the senescent soul experiences when confronted with the beauty of the other's body.

In the beautiful and painful *Casanova Homecoming* (1917), Schnitzler recounts Giacomo Casanova on the brink of old age. The famous seducer returns from his travels to spend his last days in the city of Venice. During this journey, he meets a couple of friends on the outskirts of Mantua. In their home, he is introduced to the nineteen-year-old Marcolina and the young officer Lorenzi, whom Casanova immediately discerns to be Marcolina's secret lover. Casanova is taken with desire himself and painfully envies the young man. In Schnitzler's text we discover the devilish and sordid face of masculine decline and the malicious workings of senescent desire.

While Schnitzler depicts senescence as an abyss of bitterness and cynicism, his contemporary, the Italian–Hungarian novelist Italo Svevo describes senility as a guilty and apprehensive meekness, a selfish withdrawal from the relation with the other. Svevo is the author of *Senilità* (1898), the story of a man, Emilio Brentani, who is indecisive and inactive. While not actually old, Bretani is a symbol of senility because of his hesitancy to enjoy the pleasures of life and his refusal to break out of routine or to accept the love of a young lady. A failed writer, he works as a clerk in an insurance company and lives a modest life in a shared apartment with his sister Amalia, who has few relationships in the outside world. When he meets Angiolina, a poor but beautiful woman, he tries to explain to the woman that their relationship will be subordinate to his other duties. In short, he wants to keep the relationship unofficial and for both parties to avoid commitment.

Today, old people have taken center stage for demographic reasons: they are everywhere, and they weigh down the atmosphere of everyday life with their sadness. So, in my view, senility comes to define the social landscape in a way that is unprecedented. This is the subject of *Anéantir*, a 2022 novel by Michel Houellebecq, which depicts the decline of Western society from the point of view of a French family. The book is a hopeless and irate representation of the decline of the white race and of its supremacy. But it is also a book about the agony of a family that gathers around the eighty-year-old father who has suffered a stroke.

But we should have a look at the other side of the coin of senility: lightness. The Spanish writer Sara Mesa has published some novels that treat love and affection in a more relaxed way. In *Cara de Pan* (2016), she recounts the story of a thirteen-year-old girl named Casi, who dislikes the company of her peers and prefers to stay alone in a park. Rather than going to school, she befriends an old man, who, little by little, becomes her confidant. They have nothing in common other than their lack of sociability and their taste for loneliness. The old man comes every morning to visit Casi. They speak about the sparrows in the park, the man's psychotic mother and of the mental clinic where he spent part of his life. Little by little, their friendship causes suspicion. The old man is jailed, accused of sins he did not commit. Mesa has found a different style of narration, based in irony and tenderness. In her novels, she stages stories of companionship, affection, and also erotic love between people who do not look like traditional lovers: mad people, old people, reckless children, disgruntled women. For her, old age is but one of the many oddities of the affective condition of humans.

THE COMPLETION

2023

BEFORE COMPLETION

The methodical task of writing distracts me from the present state of men. The certitude that everything has been written negates us or turns us into phantoms. I know of districts in which the young men prostrate themselves before books and kiss their pages in a barbarous manner, but they do not know how to decipher a single letter. Epidemics, heretical conflicts, peregrinations which inevitably degenerate into banditry, have decimated the population. I believe I have mentioned suicides, more and more frequent with the years. Perhaps my old age and fearfulness deceive me, but I suspect that the human species—the unique species—is about to be extinguished, but the Library will endure: illuminated, solitary, infinite, perfectly motionless, equipped with precious volumes, useless, incorruptible, secret.

—Borges, "The Library of Babel, 1941

NO HARMONY

In the above-quoted story, Borges seems to draw a picture of our present: the disintegration of human civilization, the spread of religious fanaticism among young people who kiss the pages of a book they cannot read, epidemics, conflicts, migrations that result in violence. Finally, suicides, which become more frequent every year. This is clearly a good description of the current decade.

Borges announces that the Library is not destined to disappear with humankind. It will remain—solitary, infinite, secret, and perfectly useless. Similarly, the immense library of data recorded by the countless techno-sensors installed in practically every spot on the planet will also last forever, feeding the cognitive automaton that is taking the place of frail, human organisms, poisoned by miasmas, driven to suicide. This, at least, is what Borges seems to predict.

Another prediction was made by the philosopher Francis Bacon. During the modern age, knowledge had been a factor in exerting power over nature and over other men. At a certain moment, however, the expansion of technical knowledge began to work in reverse: no longer a prosthesis of human power, technology transformed into a system endowed with an independent dynamic. We now find ourselves trapped in that dynamic.

As early as the 1960s, Günther Anders said that the power of nuclear technology would render humans powerless. States equipped with nuclear weapons would be less and less capable of escaping the logic of competition that drives an ever more destructive extension and improvement of atomic technology, developing so rapidly that even the scientists working on it didn't fully fathom it. In this functional superiority of the atomic weapon over the human, Anders saw the conditions for a new and more complete form of Nazism.

In the twenty-first century, digital technologies have created the conditions for the automation of all social interactions, making collective will almost inoperative. In his 1993 book *Out of Control: The New Biology of Machines, Social Systems, and the Economic World*, Kevin Kelly presaged as much, arguing that then-nascent digital networks would eventually create a global mind to which sub-global minds (individual or collective or institutional) would have to submit. As he was writing, research on artificial intelligence was developing. It has now reached a level of maturity sufficient to prefigure the inscription of a system of innumerable devices capable of automating human cognitive interactions onto the social body.

The logical order is inscribed in the very flows of social reproduction. But this does not mean that the social body is harmoniously regulated by it. Planetary society is increasingly filled with technical automatisms. But, as is obvious, this does not eliminate conflict, violence, or suffering. No harmony is in sight, no order seems to be established other than that of the ruling classes, which is tenuous at best.

Chaos and the automaton coexist by intertwining and feeding off each other. Chaos fuels the creation of technical interfaces of automatic control, which (re)produce value. But the proliferation of technical automatisms, challenged by the innumerable agencies of economic, political, and military power in conflict, ends up fueling the chaos rather than reducing it.

Two parallel world histories are unfolding, with ubiquitous but still disparate points of intersection: the history of geopolitical, environmental, and mental chaos on the one hand, and the history of the automatic order that is extensively concatenating on the other. Will it always be like this, or will a short circuit happen in which chaos takes over the automaton? Or will the automaton rid itself of chaos, eliminating the human agent?

THE COMPLETION

In the last pages of Dave Eggers's novel *The Circle*, Ty Gospodinov confesses his helplessness to Mae, embodied in the creature he conceived and built himself, a monstrous technological enterprise that merges Facebook, Google, PayPal, YouTube, and much more. Gospodinov remarks that he didn't want what is happening, but now it's too late. Completion, the closing of the circle, is the horizon of the novel, as technologies of capillary data collection and artificial intelligence connect perfectly in a ubiquitous network that generates a synthetic reality.

The current stage in the development of AI is probably taking us to the threshold of a leap to a dimension that I would define as a pervasive global cognitive automaton. The automaton is not an analogue of the human organism, but the convergence of innumerable devices generated by scattered artificial intelligences. The evolution of AI does not lead to the creation of androids, to the perfect simulation of the conscious organism. It rather manifests as the replacement of specific skills with pseudo-cognitive automatons that are linked together, converging in a global cognitive automaton.

In March 2023, several top tech executives, including Elon Musk and Steve Wozniak, published an open letter calling for a moratorium on advanced AI research. The letter was signed by more than a thousand senior officials from Big Tech, including Evan Sharp of Pinterest and Chris Larson of the cryptocurrency company Ripple. The letter reads in part:

> Contemporary AI systems are now becoming human-competitive at general tasks and we must ask ourselves: *Should* we let machines flood our information channels with propaganda and untruth? *Should* we automate away all the jobs, including the fulfilling ones? *Should* we develop nonhuman minds that might eventually outnumber, outsmart, obsolete and replace us? *Should* we risk loss of control of our civilization? Such decisions must not be delegated to unelected tech leaders. Powerful AI systems should be developed only once we are confident that their effects will be positive and their risks will be manageable ... Therefore, we call on all AI labs to immediately pause for at least 6 months the training of AI systems more powerful than GPT-4. This pause should be public and verifiable, and include all key actors. If such a pause cannot be enacted quickly, governments should step in and institute a moratorium.[1]

Just over a month later Geoffrey Hinton, one of the inventors of neural networks, decided to leave Google in order to express himself openly on the dangers implicit in artificial intelligence. He told the BBC that the potential of AI chatbots to become more intelligent than humans is "quite scary," noting that they could be used by "bad actors."[2] In a separate interview with *The Guardian* he said:

> [Advanced AI] will allow authoritarian leaders to manipulate their electorates ... I've come to the conclusion that the kind of intelligence we're developing is very different from the intelligence we have ... So it's as if you had 10,000

1. "Pause Giant AI Experiments: An Open Letter," *Future of Life*, March 22, 2023, https://futureoflife.org/open-letter/pause-giant-ai-experiments/, italics in original.
2. "AI 'Godfather' Geoffrey Hinton Warns of Dangers as He Quits Google," *BBC*, May 2, 2023.

> people and whenever one person learned something, everybody automatically knew it. And that's how these chatbots can know so much more than any one person.[3]

The ideological and entrepreneurial avant-garde of digital neoliberalism seems frightened by the power of the Golem. As the sorcerer's apprentices, high-tech entrepreneurs are asking for a moratorium, a pause, a period of reflection. Why? Does the invisible hand no longer work? Is capital no longer self-regulating? What is happening? What is about to happen? These are two different questions. We know, more or less, what is happening: thanks to the convergence of massive data collection, programs capable of recognition and recombination are emerging. Technology that can simulate specific intelligent skills has arrived—stochastic parrots.

What is about to happen is that stochastic parrots, thanks to their abilities to self-correct and write software, will greatly accelerate technical innovation, especially of themselves. It is assumed that what could and most likely will happen is that these innovative, self-correcting (deep-learning) devices will determine their purpose independently of their human creators. The sorcerer's apprentices are realizing that the autonomic tendency of language generators (autonomy from their human creators) is implicit in their ability to simulate human intelligence, even when confined to specific, limited skills. In other words, these specific skills will converge toward the concatenation of self-directed automata that may view their original human creators as an obstacle to be eliminated.

Why is AI causing such a stir now? In journalistic debates, caution prevails: commentators point to problems such as the dissemination of false news, the incitement of hatred, and the circulation of racist statements. This is all true and demonstrable, but not very relevant. For years, innovations in communication technology have increased verbal violence and idiocy. This cannot be what worries the masters of the automaton, those who conceived it and

3. Josh Taylor and Alex Hern, "'Godfather of AI' Geoffrey Hinton Quits Google and Warns Over Dangers of Misinformation," *The Guardian*, May 2, 2023.

are implementing it, and who are now begging for their monster to be contained.

What worries the sorcerer's apprentices, in my humble opinion, is that intelligent automatons endowed with self-correcting and self-learning behavior are destined to make decisions autonomously from their creators and to take over their elite positions. Let's think of an intelligent automaton inserted into the control section of a military device. To what extent can we be sure that it won't evolve unexpectedly, perhaps shooting its owner or, logically inferring from the data it has access to, that it should urgently launch an atomic bomb?

GENERATIVE LANGUAGE AND THOUGHT

In *The Search for the Perfect Language*, Umberto Eco writes:

> A natural language does not exist only on the basis of a syntactic and a semantics. It also lives on the basis of a pragmatics, that is, it is based on rules of use that take into account the circumstances and contexts of emission, and these same rules of use establish the possibility of rhetorical uses of the language thanks to which syntactic parts and constructions can acquire multiple meanings (as happens with metaphors).[4]

Generative pre-trained transformers (GPT) are a type of program that can respond to and converse with humans, thanks to their ability to recombine words, phrases, and images retrieved from an objectified linguistic network on the internet.

These programs have been trained on existing materials and data to recognize the meaning of words and images. They possess the ability to recognize syntax and recombine utterances, but they cannot recognize the pragmatics of living contexts, because doing so depends on the experience of a body. This experience is

4. Umberto Eco, *The Search for the Perfect Language* (John Wiley and Sons, 1997), 30.

impossible for a brain without organs. Sensitive organs constitute a source of contextual and self-reflective knowledge that the automaton does not have.

The automaton is capable of intelligence, certainly, but not of thought. The automaton is superior to humans in the field of calculation, but thought is precisely the incursion of the non-calculable (consciousness/unconscious) into knowledge and reasoning. This superiority (or, rather, this irreducibility to computation) of human thought is cold comfort, because it is of little use when it comes to interacting with computation-based generation (and destruction) devices.

From the point of view of experience, the automaton does not compete with the conscious organism. But in terms of functionality, the (pseudo-)cognitive automaton can outsmart a human agent in a specific skill (calculating, making lists, translating, aiming, shooting, and so on). The automaton is also endowed with the ability to perfect its procedures, i.e., to evolve. In other words, the cognitive automaton tends to modify the purposes of its operation, not just the procedures.

In the human sphere, language consists of signs that have meaning within an experiential context. Thanks to the pragmatic interpretation of the context, the semantic interpretation of signs (both natural and linguistic ones, endowed with intention) becomes possible. The conjunction between bodies is the nonverbal context within which the identification and disambiguation of the meaning of statements is made possible.

In the conjunctive sphere, the relationship with reality is based on the ability of language to represent and persuade. In the connective sphere, the interpretation of signs does not have the character of experience in an ambiguous context, but of recognition in the context of accuracy. Artificial linguistic intelligence consists of software capable of recognizing syntactically coherent semiotic series and of generating statements through the syntactically coherent recombination of signifying units.

Thanks to the evolution of stochastic parrots into linguistic agents capable of evolutionary self-correction, self-generating language becomes autonomous from the human agent, and the human agent is progressively wrapped up in this language. Not subsumed, but enveloped, encapsulated. Full subsumption would imply a pacification of the human, a complete acquiescence: an order, finally. A harmony, finally—albeit totalitarian. But no. War predominates in the planetary panorama.

In this neo-environment of the linguistic automaton in concatenation, human agents must perfect their connecting skills while their ability to communicate weakens and the social body stiffens and grows aggressive. The evolution of machines makes them increasingly capable of simulating humans. In this context, human evolution consists in making oneself more compatible with the machine. With this adaptation, the cognitive mutation makes the human agent more efficient in interacting with the machine, but, at the same time, less competent in communicative interaction with other human agents.

THE ETHICAL AUTOMATON IS A DELUSION

When the sorcerer's apprentices realized the implications of the self-correcting and therefore evolutionary capacity of artificial intelligence, they began to talk about the ethics of the automaton, or "alignment," as they say in their philosophical-entrepreneurial jargon. In a pompous blog post, the creators of ChatGPT declared their intention to inscribe into their products ethical criteria aligned with human values:

> Our alignment research aims to make artificial general intelligence (AGI) aligned with human values and follow human intent. We take an iterative, empirical approach: by attempting to align highly capable AI systems, we can learn what works and what doesn't, thus refining our ability to make AI systems safer and more aligned. Using scientific experiments, we study how alignment techniques scale and where they will break.[5]

5. See "Our approach to alignment research," openai.com.

But the project of inserting ethical rules into a generative machine is an old science-fictional utopia, first written about by Isaac Asimov when he formulated the three fundamental laws of robotics. Asimov himself narratively demonstrated that these laws do not work. After all, what ethical standards should we include in artificial intelligence? The experience of centuries shows that a universal agreement on ethical rules is impossible, since the criteria of ethical evaluation are related to cultural, religious, and political contexts, and also to the unpredictable pragmatic contexts of the action. There is no universal ethics. This includes the one imposed by Western domination, which in any case is starting to crack. Obviously, every artificial intelligence project will include criteria that correspond to a vision of the world, a cosmology, an economic interest, a system of values in conflict with others. Naturally, each will claim universality.

What will happen in terms of alignment will be the opposite of what is promised by the builders of the automaton: it is not the machine that aligns itself with human values, but humans who must align themselves with the automatic values of the intelligent artifact, whether it is a question of assimilating the indispensable procedures for interacting with the financial system or learning the procedures necessary to use military systems.

I don't think the self-formation process of the cognitive automaton can be corrected by law or ethical regulations. Nor can it be interrupted or deactivated. The moratorium requested by the repentant sorcerer's apprentices is not realistic. It is contrary to the internal logic of the automaton and to the historical conditions within which its self-formation is taking place—namely, economic competition and war.

In conditions of competition and war, all technical transformations that increase productive or destructive power are destined to be implemented. This means that it is no longer possible to stop the self-construction of the global automaton.

*
* *

The liberal techno-optimist Thomas Friedman wrote an opinion piece for the *New York Times* entitled "We Are Opening the Lids on Two Giant Pandora's Boxes." A sentence in the piece struck me: "'the engineering is ahead of the science to some degree,' ... That is, even the people building these so-called large language models that underlie products like ChatGPT and Bard don't fully understand how they work and the full extent of their capabilities."[6]

Where is the danger in an entity that, although it does not have human intelligence, carries out specific cognitive tasks more efficiently than humans and that can perfect its own functioning? The general function of the inorganic intelligent entity is to introduce the information order into the organism endowed with drives. The automaton has an ordering mission, but it encounters a factor of chaos along the way: the organic drive, irreducible to numerical order.

The automaton extends its dominion into ever newer fields of social action, but it fails to complete its mission as long as its expansion is limited by the persistence of the chaotic human factor. The possibility arises that, at some point, the automaton will eliminate the chaotic factor in the only possible way: by terminating human society.

We can distinguish three dimensions of reality: the existing, the possible, and the necessary. The existing (or contingent) has the character of chaos. The evolution of the existing follows the lines of the possible or those of the necessary. The possible is a projection of will and imagination. The necessary is implicit in the strength of biology and, now, also in the strength of the logical machine.

The cognitive automaton allows us to foresee the extermination of the contingent by the necessary, which naturally implies an annulment of the possible, because there is no possible without the contingency of the existent.

6. Thomas L. Friedman, "We Are Opening the Lids on Two Giant Pandora's Boxes," *New York Times*, May 2, 2023.

Leibniz's best of all possible worlds would at this point be realized, thanks to the elimination of the conscious organism that resists Logical Harmony. As always, the old adage helps us: the inevitable generally does not happen, because the unpredictable intervenes.

COLOPHON

Franco "Bifo" Berardi
Chaos and the Automaton

ISBN 978-1-5179-1710-4 (hc)
ISBN 978-1-5179-1711-1 (pb)

A Cataloging-in-Publication record for this book is available from the Library of Congress.

e-flux

Published by e-flux
www.e-flux.com
journal@e-flux.com

MINNESOTA

Printed and distributed by the
University of Minnesota Press
111 Third Avenue South
Suite 290
Minneapolis, MN 55401
www.upress.umn.edu

"Engineering Self" originally appeared in *e-flux Architecture* (December 2016).

"The Comeback of the Event as Terror and Dementia" was written in September 2018. A version of this text appears in *Big Data—A New Medium?* (Routledge, 2021) as "Simulated Replicants Forever? Big Data, Engendered Determinism, and the End of Prophecy"

"More on the American Abyss" originally appeared in *e-flux Conversations* (January 13, 2021).

"The Serpent's Egg" originally appeared in *Neuromagma* (March 2022).

"Mental Long Covid and the Techno-Social Unconscious: A Conversation with Geert Lovink" originally appeared in *e-flux notes* (May 12, 2022).

"*Unheimlich*: The Spiral of Chaos and the Cognitive Automaton" originally appeared in *e-flux Notes* (March 10, 2023).

"Sensuous Senescence" originally appeared in *Extra Extra Magazine* (May 2023).

"Cosmism and Extinction" originally appeared in *Citizens of the Cosmos* (London: Sternberg Press, 2024).

COLOPHON

SERIES EDITORS
Julieta Aranda
Kaye Cain-Nielsen
Brian Kuan Wood
Anton Vidokle

MANAGING EDITORS
Colin Beckett
Hicham Awad

DESIGN
Noah Venezia

PROOFREADER
Ciara Pattern